CABANA
THE COOKBOOK
BRASILIAN BARBECUE & BEYOND

CABANA
THE COOKBOOK
BRASILIAN BARBECUE & BEYOND

DAVID PONTE, LIZZY BARBER & JAMIE BARBER
with CHEF DAVID ROOD

PHOTOGRAPHY BY MARTIN POOLE · ILLUSTRATIONS BY ANITA MANGAN

Quadrille
PUBLISHING

for Liesbeth
DP

*for Mummy
Barber, and
George*
LB

*for Clare,
Issey and
Lola*
JB

for Jessica
DR

Editorial director: Jane O'Shea
Creative director: Helen Lewis
Project editor: Laura Gladwin
Art direction and design: Anita Mangan
Photography: Martin Poole, with Jamie Barber,
   Matthew Cooper and Josh Ponté in Brasil
Illustrations: Anita Mangan
Food stylist: Emily Quah
Props stylist: Tamzin Ferdinando
Production: James Finan

First published in 2014 by
Quadrille Publishing Limited,
Alhambra House,
27–31 Charing Cross Road,
London WC2H 0LS

www.quadrille.co.uk

Cataloguing in Publication Data: a catalogue record for
this book is available from the British Library.

UK 978 1 84949 374 1

Printed in China

This is Harold
the Llama, our
mascot at Cabana.
Harold enjoys reading,
needlework and skiing,
and would like more
friends. You can follow
him on Twitter:
@haroldcabana

CONTENTS

Like all the best things in life, Brasilian food is about sharing. Whether nibbling on tasty snacks in local bars (*botecos*), or spooning out bowls of lovingly simmered pork and bean *feijoada*, Brasilians like to enjoy food in the company of friends and family. Cooking and eating are a combined effort, and the result is all the better for it.

Traditional Brasilian food has always been rooted in home cooking; it has never been haute cuisine. It's food for nurturing. It's the food of the indigenous peoples, Portuguese colonialists, African slaves, and the multitudes of Japanese, Italians, Lebanese and Germans who have made the country their home. It makes inventive use of fresh local ingredients, such as black beans, rice, pork, prawns and countless native fruit like *açaí*, limes, many varieties of banana, cashews, coconut... the list is endless. Traditional cooking techniques focus on simple grilling and simmering to produce a range of tasty dishes that are perfect for casual communal eating. At the same time, however, restaurant gastronomy is taking root in Brasil, and many energetic young chefs are using traditional recipes and native ingredients in new and varied ways to establish a thrilling new style of cuisine.

We founded Cabana to bring our love of Brasilian food, old and new, to the wider audience it deserves. We love the tapestry of home cooking we've experienced there, but we've also been inspired by the dynamism of modern Brasilian cooking, as well as exciting new elements of what's right in front of us: the evolving face of the UK restaurant scene over the past ten or fifteen years. In this book we hope to give you the best of Cabana and the best of Brasil. From our favourite traditional barbecue dishes and comfort-food classics, to fresh, fruit-packed breakfasts and cocktails, colourful side dishes and luscious desserts, the book encompasses the results of our travels around the country as well as the discoveries we've made in the Cabana kitchen. Zingy, vibrant, fresh and full of life, this is modern Brasilian food as you've never seen it before – so invite some friends over and get cooking!

David, Jamie and Lizzy

P.S. Oh, and at Cabana, it's Brasil with an 's', just like they spell it over there.

BRASILIAN TABLE

Considering its culinary heritage, which includes, among others, African, Portuguese, Italian and Japanese cooking, you'd expect Brasilian ingredients to be exotic and unfamiliar. But with the exception of some of the indigenous fruit (see page 162), most dishes are easy to recreate at home. Here are some of the essential ingredients in any Brasilian pantry.

① BANANAS
You can usually find at least three or four different types of bananas in markets in Brasil, from firm, savoury plantains (which are breaded, fried and served as part of the *prato executivo*, or businessman's lunch) to the sweet banana *ouro*, or gold bananas, which are eaten as a snack or in cakes and puddings.

② BEANS
A classic partner to rice, slow-cooked black beans are served as a side dish or as the foundation of *feijoada*, a traditional meat and bean stew (see page 96).

③ CACHAÇA
Brasil's national spirit is made from sugar cane and can be drunk on its own, mixed in cocktails such as the classic caipirinha (see page 168), and sometimes even used as a marinade for meat or fish. Many types are available, including artisanal and matured varieties.

④ COCONUT
Milk, water, toasted or grated: you'll find coconut used in all forms throughout Brasil, from young green 'jelly' nuts drunk through a straw on Rio beaches, coconut stews in Bahia to sticky coconut desserts all over the country.

⑤ DOCE DE LEITE
Doce de leite, more commonly known by its Spanish name, *dulce de leche*, is a sticky-sweet milk-based caramel sauce that Brasilian housewives traditionally make by slowly boiling a can of condensed milk. You can use it as a breakfast spread, as a dip for fruit, or for any recipes requiring caramel or melted toffee (see page 144).

⑥ FAROFA
This cassava (also known as manioc) flour is often toasted and sprinkled over grilled meats or stews (see page 85), and provides the distinctive crunchy element in Brasilian dishes. Yoki is a well-known brand you might find in speciality Latin American shops, but if you're really stuck, breadcrumbs fried in butter can give a similar texture.

⑦ LIMES
Lemons aren't used much in Brasil – the ubiquitous citrus fruit is the *limao*, which is half way between the European lemon and the lime. They're squeezed over and into everything, from caipirinhas to crunchy rice *bolinhos* and grilled steaks. Ordinary limes are a great substitute and are easier to get hold of.

⑧ MALAGUETA CHILLI
The *malagueta* is a fiery Brasilian chilli similar to the Portuguese piri-piri. It is ubiquitous in Brasil, and you'll find a bottle or dish of them preserved in oil, vinegar or cachaça on every table top.

⑨ MATCHSTICK POTATOES
Very thin, crisp strips of potato, matchstick potatoes are very popular in Brasil. You can find them in larger supermarkets, where they're sometimes called potato sticks or straw potatoes, or in specialist Latin American shops.

⑩ RAPADURA SUGAR
Rapadura is a very basic form of sugar made from sugar cane juice that has been evaporated over a low heat, then sieved to produce a grainy brown sugar. It's also known as *panela* in Colombia, *piloncillo* in Mexico or *jaggery* in India.

⑪ RICE
As in many Latin American countries, rice is a staple of the Brasilian diet. It's served plain white (*arroz branco*), mixed with meat or with coconut, broccoli, or a variety of other ingredients.

The everyday breakfast in Brasil is usually a light and quick affair: a strong, black, super-sweet *cafezinho*, a basket of freshly baked *pão de queijo* and you're set for the day. However, there's always good cause for a big meal in Brasil, so if you're looking for something more indulgent, here's a collection of old and new breakfast dishes, from a São Paulo market special to some creations of our own, inspired by our travels.

BRASILIAN
BREAKFASTS

CORN CAKES WITH BACON & DOCE DE LEITE

SERVES 4–5

Inspired by the classic American combination of pancakes with bacon and maple syrup, our Brasilian version takes fluffy corn cakes, drizzles them with *doce de leite* (milk caramel) and tops them with grilled bacon for a luxurious brunch treat. You can also use shop-bought *dulce de leche* or condensed milk caramel.

8–10 thin smoked bacon rashers
90g plain flour
120g fine cornmeal or polenta
3 tbsp caster sugar
1 tsp baking powder
½ tsp bicarbonate of soda
½ tsp sea salt
300ml buttermilk
2 large eggs
butter, for frying
4–5 tbsp Doce de Leite (page 144), to serve

★ ★ ★ ★ ★ ★ ★ ★ ★ ★ ★ ★ ★ ★ ★ ★ ★ ★ ★ ★

Preheat the grill to medium-high. Place the bacon rashers in a single layer on a large baking tray and grill for 4–6 minutes, until golden brown and crisp. Remove and keep warm.

Place the flour, cornmeal, sugar, baking powder, bicarbonate of soda and salt a large bowl and mix well. Make a well in the centre. Whisk the buttermilk and eggs together, then pour them into the well. Gradually stir the wet ingredients into the dry until fully incorporated.

Melt a knob of butter in a large non-stick pan over a medium heat and swirl it around to coat the base of the pan. Drop in tablespoons of the corn cake batter and fry for about 2 minutes, until bubbles start to form around the edges. Flip them over and cook the other side for 1–2 minutes, until golden brown. Remove to a plate and keep warm while cooking the rest, adding a little butter each time.

Stack the corn cakes on warmed plates and drizzle over a little doce de leite. Top with the bacon rashers and serve warm.

MANGO & COCONUT GRANOLA CRUNCH

MAKES ABOUT 20 SERVINGS

This tropical granola is made from a blend of sweet dried papaya, pineapple and mango with desiccated coconut and cashews. Serve it with milk or yoghurt for a quick breakfast, or use it in our Açaí Bowl (page 20).

2 tbsp light, flavourless oil, such as sunflower, plus extra for greasing
125g maple syrup
2 tbsp runny honey
1 tsp vanilla extract
400g rolled oats
25g sunflower seeds
25g pumpkin seeds
50g toasted cashew nuts, lightly crushed
2 tsp ground cinnamon
75g desiccated coconut
175g mixed dried mango, papaya and pineapple pieces, chopped

★ ★ ★ ★ ★ ★ ★ ★ ★ ★ ★ ★ ★ ★ ★ ★ ★ ★ ★ ★

Preheat the oven to 150°C/300°F/Gas mark 2 and lightly oil a baking tray. Put the oil, maple syrup, honey, vanilla and 4 tablespoons water in a large bowl and mix well. Add the oats, seeds and cashew nuts and stir well to coat. Spread the mixture over the baking tray. Sprinkle with cinnamon and bake for 15 minutes.

Remove from the oven and stir in the coconut. Cook for another 10 minutes, until the granola is evenly golden and crisp. Remove and leave to cool completely, then stir in the dried fruit. Store in an airtight container.

COCONUT PURRIDGE

SERVES 4

This is inspired by a Brasilian sweet dish called *canjica*, which is often served at the Festa Junina, the big winter festival. *Canjica*, a type of white corn, is cooked with coconut milk and sugar, sprinkled with spices and sometimes topped with crushed peanuts. Ours is a hot version made with oats, which are much easier to get hold of. It's the perfect start to a cold day.

400ml coconut milk
400ml milk
180g rolled oats
30g desiccated coconut
4 tbsp sugar, or to taste
½ tsp ground cinnamon
½ tsp ground cloves
handful of toasted peanuts, roughly chopped
sea salt

★ ★ ★ ★ ★ ★ ★ ★ ★ ★ ★ ★ ★ ★ ★ ★ ★ ★ ★ ★

Heat the coconut milk and milk in a saucepan over a gentle heat. Add the oats, coconut, sugar and a pinch of salt and stir well. Bring to the boil, then reduce the heat and simmer gently for a few minutes, until soft and creamy. Stir in a little hot milk or boiling water if the consistency is too thick. Spoon into bowls and sprinkle over the cinnamon, cloves and chopped peanuts to serve.

SWEET POTATO HASH & MASH WITH FETA & POACHED EGGS

SERVES 4

One of the things we really pine for when we're in Brasil is a cooked breakfast with eggs, but we've been assured it doesn't exist there. 'We don't eat such a thing!', David's friend Gustavo laughed when we asked him. So we thought we'd introduce him to a little taste of our home, with a Brasilian accent. Sweet potatoes are popular at breakfast in north-eastern Brasil, and here they make a great base for poached eggs and salty crumbled feta. We'll be taking this in our suitcase next time we visit Gustavo!

4 sweet potatoes
1 tbsp sunflower oil
butter, for frying
2 tsp vinegar
4 eggs
100g feta cheese
small handful of flat-leaf parsley, chopped
1 long red chilli, deseeded and finely chopped
sea salt and freshly ground black pepper

Peel the sweet potatoes and cut two of them into small chunks. Place in a pan half-filled with salted water, bring to the boil and cook for about 10 minutes, until tender.

Meanwhile, chop the remaining sweet potatoes into 1cm cubes. Heat the oil and a knob of butter in a large heavy-based frying pan over a medium heat. Add the potato cubes and fry for 8–10 minutes, tossing occasionally, until tender and golden brown around the edges.

Drain the boiled potatoes well and mash with a potato masher. Add the mash to the frying pan and stir in the cubed potatoes. Season well with salt and pepper and stir-fry until heated through. Remove from the heat and keep warm while you cook the eggs.

Bring a large pan of water to the boil. Add the vinegar and reduce the heat to a simmer. Stir the water to make a whirlpool, then carefully crack an egg into the centre. Poach for 3–4 minutes, until set with a runny yolk. Remove with a slotted spoon and place on kitchen paper to drain. Keep warm in lukewarm water while you cook the other eggs.

Divide the potatoes between warmed plates and place a poached egg on top. Sprinkle the eggs with salt and pepper, then crumble over the feta and sprinkle with parsley and chilli. Serve immediately.

SAL
38-21-00-4

16

THE CATADORES

If you manage to snag a seat on one of Cabana's banquettes, you'll find yourself cushioned by the beautiful handiwork of two of Brasil's most innovative charitable organizations.

Da-Lata (which means 'from the can') is a UK-based company founded by Astrid Barney that works with the *catadores* of Brasil: rubbish collectors who sift through piles of discarded material and turn them into other things. Da-Lata helps turn empty soft-drink cans into unique fashion and home accessories. They collect the ring pulls from cans (which are then recycled), then clean and polish them up for female Brasilian artisans to crochet into jewellery, handbags, cushions and table mats. During the past three years, Da-Lata has also started running training programmes in a women's prison in the outskirts of the capital, Brasília, to give the inmates an income and a skill to take away when they leave. The colourful cushions on Cabana's banquettes are each painstakingly made by Da-Lata from more than 2,000 ring pulls, and we're proud to support a project which creates something so positive, literally out of the scrap heap.

Recicla Jeans is a project founded by Nadia Rubio Bacchi to give the women of Paraisópolis, the second-largest *favela* in São Paulo, a source of income. The project helps around 30 women create clothing and accessories from recycled jeans. Since it was founded three years ago, their work has already been exported as far as Italy, Spain and Portugal. The jeans banquettes at Cabana are the first upholstery they have worked on, and we're delighted to be able to showcase their work in the restaurant, where it's a great reminder of the creativity that can come out of the 'upcycling' ethos.

AÇAÍ BOWL

SERVES 3–4 (MAKES 500ML)

When São Paulo's Mercado Municipal stirs into life at 6.00 a.m. you'll often find Paulistas fuelling their morning shopping with an *açaí* bowl from a fruit or juice stall. This powerhouse breakfast features Brasil's most famous superfood: *açaí* (pronounced 'ah-sigh-ee'), a bright purple berry from the Amazon that's gaining worldwide attention for its antioxidant and energy-boosting properties. If you can't find the pulp you can freeze store-bought mixed smoothies made with *açaí* juice, in which case you'll probably need less apple or orange juice. Decant the smoothie into a sealable plastic bag and leave in the freezer for three hours, or overnight.

250g frozen açaí pulp
4 large ripe bananas, peeled and sliced
75–100ml orange or apple juice
6–8 tbsp Mango & Coconut Granola Crunch (page 14)
200g strawberries, hulled and sliced

★ ★ ★ ★ ★ ★ ★ ★ ★ ★ ★ ★ ★ ★ ★ ★ ★ ★ ★ ★

Break up the frozen açaí pulp while it's still in its packaging. Open the packet and put the pulp in a blender with 2 sliced bananas. Add a splash of juice and blend at high speed until you get a purée with the consistency of a soft sorbet. If you prefer it thinner, add a touch more juice and blend again. Pour into individual bowls and sprinkle over the granola. Top with sliced strawberries and the remaining sliced bananas and serve immediately.

BRASILIAN HOT CHOCOLATE

SERVES 4–6

It's no secret that Brasilians have sweet teeth, and this hot chocolate is practically a dessert in itself. The condensed milk gives it a rich, caramel-like flavour and the spices provide a subtle warmth.

200g condensed milk
4–5 tbsp good-quality unsweetened cocoa powder, or to taste
pinch of sea salt
pinch of ground cinnamon
pinch of freshly grated nutmeg
pinch of ground ginger
pinch of ground cloves

★ ★ ★ ★ ★ ★ ★ ★ ★ ★ ★ ★ ★ ★ ★ ★

Put the condensed milk, cocoa, salt and ground spices in a saucepan. Slowly stir in 1 litre hot water until evenly combined. Put the pan over a medium heat and bring to a gentle simmer, stirring occasionally. (The hot milk can easily boil over, so do not leave the pan unattended). Taste a little to check the sweetness – add a splash of boiling water if you prefer it less sweet. Ladle into mugs and serve immediately. Any leftovers can be covered and refrigerated for up to 5 days, ready to be reheated.

RABANADAS

SERVES 4–6

Originally from Portugal, *rabanadas* are a kind of Brasilian French toast that often appear on breakfast tables at Christmas. The bread is soaked in condensed milk, then fried until crispy, with a custard-like, melt-in-the-mouth texture on the inside. The sweet wine that was originally used is now more often replaced with milk. It's a rich breakfast treat that's good enough to eat all year round.

1 sourdough baguette
3 eggs
100ml whole milk
175g sweetened condensed milk
½ tsp vanilla extract
½ tsp sea salt
butter, for frying
1 tbsp unsweetened cocoa powder
1 tbsp ground cinnamon
1 tbsp icing sugar
fresh berries, to serve (optional)
Greek yoghurt or Doce de Leite (page 144),
     to serve (optional)

Slice the baguette diagonally into 2–2.5cm-thick slices and arrange them in a single layer in a wide, shallow baking dish. Beat the eggs lightly in a bowl, then whisk in the milk, condensed milk, vanilla extract and salt. Pour the mixture over the bread, then turn the slices over and press down to ensure they are well coated. Cover with clingfilm and chill for 20–30 minutes.

Just before eating, melt the butter in a large non-stick pan over a medium heat. Use a fork to lift each bread slice to allow the excess liquid to drip away, then lower it into the pan. Fry them in batches for about 2 minutes on each side, until golden brown. Remove to a tray and keep warm.

Meanwhile, mix the cocoa powder, cinnamon and icing sugar together. Dust it over just before serving. Serve warm, with fresh berries and Greek yoghurt or doce de leite, if you like.

Whenever you walk into a *boteco* (bar) in Brasil, you'll find yourself presented with a list of *salgadinhos* – literally 'little salty things' – to nibble alongside your beer or cocktail. Some places, such as Aconchego Carioca in downtown Rio, do a variety of different things very well, while others pride themselves on their skill at one snack: Bar do Adão in Leblon has a list of more than 30 *pastels* (pastries), each with a different mouthwatering filling. They're best enjoyed with plenty of friends and a cold drink, but also make a perfect starter for a barbecue or dinner party. Make a few different ones, put them in the middle of the table and see how long it takes for the plates to empty!

BAR SNACKS, STARTERS & STREET FOOD

COXINHAS

Coxinha means 'little drumstick', and refers to the shape of these tasty chicken croquettes. If you asked twenty Brasilians for their recipe you'd receive a different one every time: some are made with potato, some with cheese, and some with a real chicken drumstick encased in batter. Ours are made with shredded chicken and spices, and are delicious on their own or dipped in Molho Vinagrete (page 85) or our Chilli Mayonnaise (page 86).

2 boneless, skinless chicken breasts (300–350g)
450g floury potatoes, quartered
2 tbsp olive oil
1 large onion, finely chopped
4 tbsp Spicy Malagueta Marinade (page 88)
100g plain flour
2 eggs, lightly beaten
100g panko breadcrumbs
vegetable oil, for deep-frying
few sprigs of flat-leaf parsley, finely chopped
sea salt and freshly ground black pepper

Bring a small pan of salted water to the boil, then reduce the heat to a simmer. Add the chicken and poach very gently for 10 minutes (only a few bubbles should break the surface). Remove from the heat, cover and leave to continue cooking in the residual heat for 10–15 minutes, until cooked through and firm when lightly squeezed. Remove from the liquid and leave to cool, reserving the poaching liquid.

Bring the poaching liquid to the boil and add the potatoes. Simmer for 10–15 minutes, until just tender. Drain well, then leave in the pan to dry out before mashing. Season with salt and pepper.

Meanwhile, heat the olive oil in a small pan, add the onion and cook gently, stirring, over a medium-low heat for 8–10 minutes, until soft and translucent.

To assemble, shred the chicken into small pieces and place in a large bowl. Add the mashed potatoes, onions and Spicy Malagueta Marinade. Mix well, then taste and season with salt and pepper. With damp hands, shape about 50g of the mixture into a drumstick shape, like a teardrop with a rounded base and pointed top. Set it upright on a plate and repeat with the rest of the mixture. Coat each one in flour, then egg, then breadcrumbs. Cover with clingfilm and chill for at least an hour to firm up.

Heat the oil in a deep-fryer to 170°C/325°F. Fry in batches for 3–4 minutes, turning once or twice, until golden brown. Remove and drain on kitchen paper. Serve warm, sprinkled with chopped parsley and a little more sea salt, if you like.

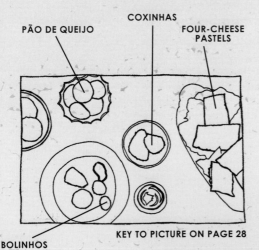

PÃO DE QUEIJO

COXINHAS

FOUR-CHEESE PASTELS

BOLINHOS

KEY TO PICTURE ON PAGE 28

PÃO DE QUEIJO

MAKES 25–30

Crispy puffs of dough with a mild, cheesy flavour, *pão de queijo* are eaten for breakfast or as a snack all over Brasil. The secret to this addictive treat is the use of cassava flour (*polvilho azedo*), which gives the balls an irresistibly moist, chewy texture. The best ones we've ever tasted were from a tiny hole-in-the-wall bakery in São Paulo, and we like to think this recipe comes pretty close.

125ml whole milk
50ml vegetable oil
1 tsp sea salt
250g cassava flour (or substitute tapioca flour)
2 eggs, lightly beaten
200g Parmesan or mature Cheddar cheese, grated

★ ★ ★ ★ ★ ★ ★ ★ ★ ★ ★ ★ ★ ★ ★ ★ ★ ★ ★ ★

Put 125ml water, the milk, vegetable oil and salt in a large pan and bring to the boil. As soon as it rises up the sides of the pan, remove it from the heat. Quickly tip in the flour and stir vigorously to combine. Keep stirring until the mixture comes together as a wet dough and comes away from the side of the pan. Transfer to the bowl of a stand mixer and leave to cool slightly.

Once slightly cooled, add the eggs and start mixing at a low speed. After 1–2 minutes, increase the speed to high and beat vigorously until all the egg has been incorporated and the dough is smooth. Add the Parmesan and keep beating until the cheese is evenly mixed in.

Line a baking sheet with silicone liner or baking parchment. With damp or lightly oiled hands, roll tablespoons of the dough into small balls, about 25–30g each. You may need to wash your hands occasionally, as the dough is quite sticky. (If you have one, use a small ice-cream scoop to make this easier. Dip the scoop briefly in water, then flick away any excess water before scooping each ball). Arrange the balls 2.5cm apart on the prepared baking sheet. You can prepare them a few hours ahead and put the tray in the fridge until you're ready to bake.

Preheat the oven to 200°C/400°F/Gas mark 6. Bake for 20–25 minutes, until puffed up and evenly golden brown. They should have a crisp exterior and a doughy, chewy centre. Serve immediately.

PÃO DE QUEIJO IN SÃO PAULO

FOUR-CHEESE PASTELS

MAKES 24–26

Brasil has the largest Japanese community outside Japan, but because the two countries were once at war, many Japanese immigrants tried to pass as Chinese, cooking their native dishes with a Chinese accent. The *pastel* (originating from the spring roll) is one such dish, and is still enjoyed all over the country.

VARIATIONS

Prawn & Palm Heart Pastels

Melt 2 tablespoons butter in a pan, add a finely chopped onion and 3 chopped garlic cloves and cook gently for a few minutes. Skin, deseed and finely chop 2 tomatoes and add to the pan with 1 tablespoon tomato purée. Stir well and cook for a few minutes until the onions are soft. Drain and roughly chop a 400g tin of palm hearts. Roughly chop 100g cooked, peeled prawns. Add to the pan and season well with salt and pepper. Allow to cool before filling the pastels as described in the recipe.

Beef Pastels

Heat 2 tablespoons olive oil in a wide pan, add 400g minced beef and cook until browned. Add 1 finely chopped spring onion, 2 chopped garlic cloves and 2 peeled, deseeded and chopped tomatoes. Fry for a few more minutes until the tomatoes have softened. Remove from the heat, season with salt and pepper and stir in 2 tablespoons chopped parsley. Allow to cool before filling the pastels as described in the recipe.

500g plain flour, plus extra for dusting
1½ tsp fine sea salt
1 tbsp hot chicken stock (or water)
15g lard, melted
1 tbsp cachaça
100g grated Gruyère cheese
100g cream cheese
100g feta cheese, crumbled
100g ricotta
½ tsp freshly ground black pepper
vegetable or groundnut oil, for deep-frying
Molho Vinagrete, to serve (page 85)
Mango Salsa, to serve (page 86)

★ ★ ★ ★ ★ ★ ★ ★ ★ ★ ★ ★ ★ ★ ★ ★ ★ ★ ★ ★

First, make the dough. Put the flour and salt in a large bowl and mix well. Make a well in the centre. Stir the stock, lard, cachaça and 125ml warm water in a jug, then pour this into the well. Stir together to form a soft dough. If it's too dry and won't form a ball, gradually add more warm water until it comes together. Tip the mixture on to a lightly floured surface and knead briefly until smooth. Do not overwork it, or it will become tough. Cover with clingfilm and set aside for at least 15 minutes.

Mix together the four cheeses and black pepper in a small bowl and line a baking sheet with baking parchment. On a lightly floured surface, roll out half the dough very thinly (cover the other half in clingfilm), then cut out 10cm squares. Put 1 teaspoon filling in the centre of each square on one side. Brush a little water around the edges, then fold over the other half to make a rectangle. Press down on the edges to seal, trying not to create any air pockets. Use the tines of a fork to press down along all four sides to ensure a good seal. Continue making the rest of the pastels, transferring them to the baking sheet.

Heat the oil in a deep-fryer to 180°C/350°F. Fry in batches for 3–4 minutes, until golden brown on both sides, turning them halfway. Drain on kitchen paper and keep warm while you fry the rest. Serve warm with Molho Vinagrete or Mango Salsa, if you like.

30

BOLINHOS

MAKES 20–25

Bolinhos are a mainstay of Brasil's bar scene.
They're little balls of rice that are lightly fried
for a golden crunch, which gives way to a soft,
almost creamy interior. We've incorporated
the cooking of the rice into the recipe, but
leftover rice can also be used. If it's quite dry,
you might need to add an extra egg to help it
to stick together.

150g long-grain rice
1 egg, lightly beaten
4 spring onions, trimmed and finely chopped
70g Parmesan cheese, grated, plus extra
    for sprinkling
1 tsp sea salt, or to taste
1 tsp baking powder
about 80g plain flour, plus extra for rolling
small bunch of flat-leaf parsley, finely chopped
vegetable or groundnut oil, for deep-frying
lime wedges, to serve (optional)

★ ★ ★ ★ ★ ★ ★ ★ ★ ★ ★ ★ ★ ★ ★ ★

First, cook the rice. Put it in a pan with
400ml water and bring to the boil. Reduce
the heat and simmer, part-covered, for about
10 minutes, until most of the water has been
absorbed. Remove, cover and leave to steam
for another few minutes. It will be slightly
overcooked and sticky, and you should be able
to shape it easily. Set aside to cool completely.

Add the egg, spring onions, Parmesan, salt,
baking powder, half the flour and the chopped
parsley (reserving 1 tablespoon) to the rice.
Mix well and check the consistency: it should
be stiff enough to shape into balls. If it's too
sticky, gradually add more flour until you
get the right consistency. With well-floured
hands, roll into walnut-sized balls, about
30g each.

Heat the oil in a deep-fryer to 180°C/350°F
(it should sizzle when a little rice mixture is
added to it). Fry in batches for 2–3 minutes,
until golden brown all over, then drain on
kitchen paper. Keep warm while you fry
the remaining batches. To serve, transfer
to warmed bowls and serve sprinkled with
grated Parmesan and the remaining parsley,
and lime wedges alongside.

BOLINHOS DE BACALHAU

MAKES 40–45

There are many variations of *bolinhos*, but the
best known is the *bolinho de bacalhau*. Salt cod is
a big staple of Brasilian food – it's even served
as one of the main dishes on Christmas Day.

300g salt cod
300g dry mashed potatoes (with no
    milk or butter)
small handful of flat-leaf parsley,
    finely chopped
2–3 spring onions, finely chopped
3 eggs, separated
vegetable or groundnut oil, for deep-frying
sea salt and freshly ground black pepper
lime wedges, to serve
Chilli Mayonnaise (page 86), to serve

★ ★ ★ ★ ★ ★ ★ ★ ★ ★ ★ ★ ★ ★ ★ ★

De-salt the salt cod by soaking and rinsing it
in 4–5 changes of cold water. If possible, do
this over 24 hours. Drain and place it in
a saucepan with enough cold water to cover.
Bring to a simmer and gently poach for
5 minutes, until soft. Drain and leave to cool
for a few minutes, then flake the fish and
discard any skin or bones.

Put the flaked cod in a large bowl and add the
mashed potatoes, parsley, spring onions and
egg yolks. Mix well and season with salt and
pepper. In a large, clean bowl, whisk the egg
whites to stiff peaks, then fold them into the
cod mixture.

Heat the oil in a deep-fryer to 180°C/350°F.
If you have one, use a mini ice-cream scoop
to carefully drop rough balls of cod mixture
into the hot oil. Alternatively, drop in rounded
teaspoons of the mixture. Fry for 1½–2½
minutes until golden brown, then turn over
and cook the other side. Remove and drain on
kitchen paper. Keep warm while you fry the
remaining batches.

Serve warm with lime wedges and
Chilli Mayonnaise.

31

PULLED PORK SLIDERS

SERVES 4 AS A MAIN COURSE

Sliders are mini hamburgers, which are popular in the States, and here's our Brasilian take on them. The pulled pork is really worth the effort, and it's also used in *feijoada* (see page 96). It's even better finished on the barbecue: once cooked, add more spice mix and brown sugar, then barbecue until lightly caramelized around the edges.

For the pulled pork
1 tsp sea salt
1 tsp dried oregano
½ tsp caster sugar
2 tbsp ground black pepper
50g soft dark brown sugar
1 tsp cayenne pepper
1 tbsp sweet paprika
2 tbsp smoked paprika
1 tsp garlic powder
1¼ tbsp celery salt
2 tsp ground coriander
800g–1kg pork shoulder

For the sliders
12 freshly baked Pão de Queijo (page 27)
3½ tbsp Spicy Malagueta Marinade (page 88)
handful of flat-leaf parsley, finely chopped

Preheat the oven to 140°C/275°F/Gas mark 1. First, mix together all the ingredients except the pork in a bowl, then transfer to a clean, sealable jar. Any leftover spice mix will keep well.

Remove the rind and trim off any excess fat from the pork, then put it in a roasting pan and rub in 2–3 tablespoons of the spice mix, making sure it is evenly coated. Cover with kitchen foil and roast for 7–8 hours, until the pork is very tender and you can pull it apart with a fork. Remove and leave it to cool a little. Pull the pork into shreds with a fork or slice it thinly and moisten the meat with the juices in the pan. Any leftovers will freeze beautifully.

To assemble the sliders, slice the Pão de Queijo in half horizontally. If using leftover buns, halve and toast them before using. Mix the pork with the Spicy Malagueta Marinade and add a spoonful to each base. Top with the remaining halves and serve 3 sliders per person, sprinkled with parsley.

CHICKEN EMPADINHAS

MAKES ABOUT 36

Empanadas and *empadinhas* (little ones) are savoury pies found in bars and buffet tables throughout Brasil. Traditionally, an olive is placed in the centre – the origin of the expression *a azeitona da empanada* ('an olive in the *empanada*'), which refers to something that is the crucial element. *Catupiry* is a Brasilian soft cream cheese, but it's hard to find, so you can substitute ordinary cream cheese. You can also replace the chicken with chopped canned palm hearts for a vegetarian version.

225g soft butter
450g plain flour, sifted
1¾ tsp sea salt
2 large eggs, lightly beaten
2 tbsp olive oil
1 shallot, finely chopped
2 garlic cloves, finely crushed
1 plum tomato, deseeded and finely chopped
1 tbsp tomato purée
50g peas, thawed if frozen
200g skinless and boneless cooked chicken, chopped
1 tbsp chopped flat-leaf parsley
1 tbsp chopped coriander
1 spring onion, finely chopped
pinch of ground nutmeg
100g catupiry or cream cheese
2 egg yolks mixed with 2 tbsp olive oil, to glaze
sea salt and freshly ground black pepper

★ ★ ★ ★ ★ ★ ★ ★ ★ ★ ★ ★ ★ ★ ★ ★ ★ ★ ★

First, make the pastry. Put the butter in a stand mixer and beat until pale and light. Add the flour and salt and mix at low speed until combined. Gradually add the egg, mixing until the pastry starts to come together. Try to shape an olive-sized ball of dough – if it's too dry, add 1 tablespoon cold water and mix again. Gather it into a ball, flatten it slightly, wrap it in clingfilm and chill in the fridge.

Heat the olive oil in a pan over a medium heat. Add the shallot and cook for 4–6 minutes, stirring, until soft but not browned. Add the garlic and cook for 30 seconds, until fragrant. Stir in the tomato and tomato purée and cook for 2–3 minutes. Take the pan off the heat. Mix in the rest of the ingredients except the cream cheese and season with salt and pepper. Transfer to a large bowl and leave to cool before folding in the cream cheese. It should be moist and juicy, but not runny.

Preheat the oven to 180°C/350°F/Gas mark 4 and lightly butter three 12-hole mini pie or muffin tins. Roll out the dough to 3mm thick on a lightly floured surface. Use a round pastry cutter 2–3cm larger than the diameter of the holes in the tin to cut out 36 pastry circles. Press them into the prepared tins, leaving a little dough sticking out around the edge. Brush the base and sides with the egg and oil glaze. Place 1 teaspoon filling into each one. Roll out the remaining pastry and cut out 36 rounds slightly bigger than the diameter of the pies. Cover the pies with the rounds, pressing the edges together to seal. Trim off any excess dough. Brush the tops with the glaze and bake for 20–25 minutes, until golden brown. Remove and cool slightly before turning out. Serve warm.

34

TUDO BEM TALES

Tudo bem means 'everything's good'. It's a typically Brasilian expression that sums up an optimistic approach to life. The *tudo bem* spirit has been a great influence in creating Cabana, and along our journey we've found some great stories that showcase this positive philosophy. Here are some of our favourites.

THE BICICLOTECA

Collecting and distributing books to disadvantaged areas can present logistical problems, but the Institute of Green Mobility in Brasil has found a simple solution in the Bicicloteca, a pedal-powered tricycle that has been converted into a mobile library.

The tricycle was created to take books to homeless people who have no access to a library or education, or those who can't afford books. It can navigate hard-to-reach places without the need for a driving licence or fuel and has the capacity to carry 150kg of donated books. Each one is stamped to remind the reader to pass it on, thereby creating a continuous cycle of reading and lending.

BRASILIAN OBAMAS

During the 2012 municipal elections in Brasil, hopeful candidates running for office thought they might be able get some of Barack Obama's electoral success to rub off on them by incorporating his name into their own. There were several Baracks in the running, and a few even adopted Obama as a surname, hoping that the positivity of Obama's image would inspire electorates to vote for them. These aren't the only ways candidates have tried to stand out, though: they've been known to dress up in costumes as a range of characters to inspire voters, from Santa Claus to Batman. Even Brasil's most famous leader, President Luiz Inácio Lula da Silva, ran for office using his nickname, Lula, which is Portuguese for squid. If only our elections were this colourful!

O CÉU DA BANDEIRA – THE SKY OF THE FLAG

According to Brasilian tradition, the stars on the national flag represent the constellation that appeared in the night sky on the day of the creation of the Brasilian republic on 15 November 1889. The 27 stars represent the Brasilian states and the Federal District. The constellation of the Southern Cross is on the meridian. To the south is Polaris, representing the Federal District. The motto appears on a band that roughly coincides with the ecliptic (the path of the sun). A single star lies above the band, representing the large northern state of Pará, which straddles the Equator.

TOASTED GIANT CORN

SERVES 6–8 AS A SNACK

This is great served with drinks as an alternative to nuts or olives. Dried giant white corn is available from South American grocers.

300g dried giant white corn (hominy)
2 tbsp vegetable oil
2 tsp sea salt
1 tsp smoked paprika

Soak the corn in a bowl of cold water for at least 12 hours or overnight. Drain and spread out to dry on a tray lined with a clean tea towel for at least 1 hour.

Heat the oil in a heavy-based frying pan over a medium heat. When the oil is hot but not smoking, add the corn kernels and toss until evenly coated with oil. Cover with a lid and cook for 10 minutes, shaking the pan occasionally, until the kernels are evenly golden and some of them have popped. If the kernels are still a bit chewy, toast them in an oven preheated to 150°C/300°F/Gas mark 2 for 10–20 minutes, stirring a few times. Remove and toss with a little salt and paprika. Leave to cool and store in an airtight container, if not serving immediately.

FOUR-CORN SALAD

SERVES 4–5 AS A STARTER OR SIDE

This light, refreshing salad combines four different types of corn: sweet, giant, toasted and on the cob, along with tender palm hearts and our tangy house dressing. It's delicious on its own as a starter, or alongside grilled chicken, meat or fish for a healthy dinner. You can adjust the ratios of the different corns according to what you have to hand – for example you can substitute ordinary tinned sweetcorn for the giant white corn, if it's difficult to find.

100g tinned giant white corn, drained (optional)
1 corn cob
195g tinned sweet corn, drained
100g tinned hearts of palm, drained and thinly sliced
handful of Toasted Giant Corn, about 30–50g (see left)
handful of flat-leaf parsley, finely chopped
1 tsp Cabana's Simple Dressing (page 85)
sea salt and freshly ground black pepper

Taste the giant white corn. Some people find it too chewy; if you do, blanch it in simmering salted water for 10–20 minutes, until tender. Otherwise, set aside.

Heat a griddle pan over a high heat until hot. Griddle the corn cob, turning it occasionally, until charred and blackened around the edges. Using a sharp knife, hold the cob upright on a chopping board and slice the kernels off in large chunks. Place the corn kernels in a bowl with the giant white corn and add the remaining ingredients. Season well with salt and pepper. It's best to serve the salad soon after assembling, or the toasted corn may lose its crunch.

BLACK BEAN SOUP SHOT

This thick soup of black turtle beans, known as *caldinho de feijão* in Portuguese, is an instant shot of warmth on a cold day. We serve ours in little espresso cups topped with crème fraîche and bacon, but it's equally delicious as a starter in a large bowl or mug.

2 tbsp olive oil
1 onion, chopped
1 garlic clove, chopped
½ red chilli, deseeded and chopped
1 small carrot, chopped
1 celery stick, chopped
1 leek, trimmed and chopped
1 tbsp tomato purée
1 x 400g tin black turtle beans, drained
1 heaped tsp powdered vegetable bouillon, or 1 vegetable stock cube
1 sprig thyme, leaves stripped
sea salt and freshly ground black pepper
crème fraîche, crispy bacon lardons and finely chopped flat-leaf parsley, to serve (optional)

★ ★ ★ ★ ★ ★ ★ ★ ★ ★ ★ ★ ★ ★ ★ ★ ★

Heat the oil in a large pan, add the chopped vegetables and season with salt and pepper. Cook over a medium-low heat, stirring occasionally, for about 10 minutes, until softened but not coloured. Add the tomato purée and stir again. Cook for a few more minutes, then add the beans, vegetable bouillon, thyme and hot water to cover. Bring to a simmer and cook gently for 10–15 minutes, until very soft.

Carefully transfer the soup to a blender and purée until smooth. If the soup is too thick, add a splash of boiling water and blend again. Season well with salt and pepper. Serve immediately or leave to cool and store in the fridge. Reheat the soup, if necessary, and serve in warmed bowls (or espresso cups, if serving as soup shots) with a little crème fraîche, crispy bacon lardons and a sprinkling of chopped parsley, if you like.

SWEETCORN SOUP SHOT

The Portuguese colonists couldn't grow wheat in the tropical North East, so indigenous crops such as cassava and corn became a much-used substitute. Corn and cornmeal feature in many dishes from sweet desserts to savoury starters, such as this hearty soup.

20g butter
1 leek, white part only, roughly chopped
1 small onion, roughly chopped
1 celery stick, roughly chopped
200g fresh or thawed frozen sweetcorn
1 heaped tsp powdered vegetable bouillon or 1 vegetable stock cube
sea salt and freshly ground black pepper
crème fraîche, Molho Vinagrete (page 85) and finely chopped flat-leaf parsley, to serve (optional)

Melt the butter in a heavy-based pan and add the leek, onion and celery. Cook over a medium-low heat for 8–10 minutes, stirring occasionally, until softened. Add the sweetcorn and pour in enough boiling water to cover. Stir in the vegetable bouillon powder and bring to a simmer. Cook for another 10–15 minutes, until the vegetables are very soft and tender.

Carefully transfer the soup to a blender and purée until smooth. Return the soup to the pan and season well with salt and pepper. Serve immediately or leave to cool and store in the fridge.

Reheat the soup, if necessary, and serve in warmed bowls (or espresso cups, if serving as soup shots) with a little crème fraîche, Molho Vinagrete and a sprinking of chopped parsley, if you like.

SANDRA'S PRAWN SOUP

SERVES 4

When we told our family and friends we were planning to write a cookbook, David's Brasilian godmother Sandra passed on her own collection of family recipes as a source of inspiration. We thought this recipe was absolutely delicious and we had to share it with you. So thank you, Sandra!

450g raw king prawns
20g butter
1 small onion, finely chopped
1 celery stick, finely chopped
1 carrot, finely chopped
50g white or chestnut mushrooms, chopped
¼–½ tsp cayenne pepper
75ml dry white wine
200ml double cream
1 tbsp olive oil
1 tbsp finely chopped flat-leaf parsley
sea salt

★ ★ ★ ★ ★ ★ ★ ★ ★ ★ ★ ★ ★ ★ ★ ★ ★ ★ ★ ★

Remove the shells from the prawns, put the shells in a pan and cover with cold water. Bring to the boil. Reduce the heat and simmer for 20 minutes, then strain and reserve the liquid, discarding the shells.

Meanwhile, devein the prawns and reserve 12 for the garnish. Chop the rest into small pieces. Cover with clingfilm and chill.

Melt the butter in a large, heavy-based pan over a medium heat, add the vegetables and cook for 6–8 minutes, stirring frequently, until softened. Season with salt and a little cayenne pepper. Add the wine and let it boil until reduced by half. Pour in the prawn stock and bring to a simmer. Cook gently for 10–15 minutes, then add the double cream and bring back to a simmer. Finally, add the chopped prawns and cook for 2–3 minutes, until just cooked through. Remove from the heat.

Heat the oil in a frying pan until hot and add the reserved whole prawns. Season with salt and a little more cayenne pepper and fry for 2–3 minutes, tossing once or twice, until they turn pink and opaque and are just cooked through.

Ladle the prawn soup into warmed bowls and garnish with the fried whole prawns and a sprinkling of chopped parsley and cayenne pepper. Serve immediately.

SALMON CEVICHE

SERVES 4–5

Ceviche (pronounced 'see-vee-chay') is raw fish marinated in citrus juice and seasoned with chilli. It's a popular lunch for busy city workers in São Paulo, along with sushi and sashimi. Ours is marinated in orange and lime juice and seasoned with chopped red chillies – a perfect light starter for a summer evening.

400–450g very fresh, boneless, skinless salmon fillet (ask for sashimi-grade salmon)
3 tbsp freshly squeezed lime juice
3 tbsp freshly squeezed orange juice
1 small red chilli, deseeded and finely chopped
1 tbsp finely chopped flat-leaf parsley
sea salt
lime wedges, to serve

To get nice, even slices, freeze the salmon fillet for about 30 minutes until it is very cold and quite firm. Use a sharp knife to slice the salmon thinly at an angle. Try to cut each slice with a long single stroke and aim for it to be no more than 5mm thick. Arrange the slices neatly on a serving plate. If not serving immediately, cover with clingfilm and chill in the fridge.

About 20–30 minutes before you're ready to serve, remove the salmon from the fridge and let it come to room temperature. Dress with the lime and orange juices, then sprinkle the chilli, parsley and salt over the top. Garnish with the lime wedges and serve.

SWEET POTATO CRAB CAKES

MAKES 8

Crab cakes and fritters are wildly popular along the coast of Brasil, especially in Pelourinho, the historic centre of Salvador, Bahia. Ours have plenty of fresh crab meat, sweet potato and lime juice – a real taste of tropical Brasil.

250g or 1 large sweet potato
250g fresh white crab meat
½ green pepper, deseeded and finely chopped
½ small red onion, peeled and finely chopped
50g fresh breadcrumbs
handful of flat-leaf parsley, finely chopped
1 tbsp lime juice
1 tbsp good-quality mayonnaise
¼ tsp freshly ground black pepper
75g dried breadcrumbs
vegetable oil, for frying
sea salt and freshly ground black pepper
lime wedges, to serve
Mango Salsa (page 86), to serve

Preheat the oven to 180°C/350°F/Gas mark 4. Prick the sweet potato with a fork and wrap it in kitchen foil. Bake for 45 minutes, until soft. Remove and leave to cool slightly.

Pick through the crabmeat and remove any bits of shell. Set aside in the fridge.

Peel the potato and put the flesh in a large bowl. Mash it with a fork or potato masher. Add the pepper, onion, fresh breadcrumbs, parsley, lime juice and mayonnaise and season with salt and pepper. Mix well, then fold through the crab meat. Divide the mixture into 8, then shape each portion into a round patty and coat it with the dried breadcrumbs. Place on a tray, cover with clingfilm and chill for at least 20 minutes, until they have firmed up slightly.

When ready to cook, heat enough oil to shallow-fry the crab cakes in a large pan over a medium heat. Fry in batches for 2–4 minutes on each side, until golden brown. Remove and drain on kitchen paper. Keep warm while frying the rest. Serve warm with Mango Salsa and lime wedges on the side.

(KIBE)

MAKES 25–30

Having been brought over by the small Lebanese community, beef and bulgur wheat balls, or *kibe*, are a wonderful illustration of Brasil's mixed culinary heritage.

150g bulgur wheat
1 tbsp vegetable or sunflower oil
1 small onion, finely chopped
3–4 garlic cloves, finely chopped
500g good-quality lean minced beef
1 tbsp finely chopped flat-leaf parsley
1 tbsp finely chopped mint
vegetable or groundnut oil, for deep-fat frying
sea salt and freshly ground black pepper
lime wedges, to serve
Chilli Mayonnaise, Mango Salsa or Molho Vinagrete (page 85–6), to serve

Place the bulgur wheat in a large bowl and pour over 250ml boiling water. Cover and leave to stand for 30–45 minutes, until all the water has been absorbed.

Heat the oil in a large non-stick frying pan over a medium heat. Add the onion and half the garlic and cook for a few minutes, until softened. Season a third of the minced beef with salt and pepper and add to the pan. Break up any large chunks and cook, stirring frequently, over a high heat until the moisture has evaporated. Set aside and leave to cool.

Put the remaining beef mince in a food processor. Add the bulgur wheat, parsley, mint, remaining garlic and season with salt and pepper. Blend to a paste. Cook a little and taste it to check the seasoning, adjusting if needed. Line a large baking tray with baking parchment. Moisten your hands, take a tablespoon (about 30g) of the raw mince paste and shape it into a ball. Holding it in one hand, use the other one to make a hole in it. Fill the pocket with the cooked mince, then seal and shape it into a small rugby ball. Place on the tray and repeat with the rest of the mixture.

Heat the oil in a deep-fryer to 170°C/325°F. Fry in batches until dark brown and crisp. Remove and drain on kitchen paper, then serve warm with lime wedges and sauces to dip.

LINGUIÇA IN CACHAÇA

SERVES 4 AS A SNACK

Linguiça is a spicy garlic sausage that's popular in most Portuguese-speaking countries. We've substituted chorizo here, which has the same cured flavour but is easier to get hold of. It's a dish that David fondly remembers enjoying at bars in Rio along with a *chopp*, an extra-cold beer served in small glasses so it doesn't get warm too quickly.

4 soft, fresh chorizo sausages
4 tbsp olive oil
3–4 tbsp cachaça
2 large onions, thinly sliced
4 garlic cloves, thinly sliced
handful of chives, finely chopped

Thinly slice the chorizo on the diagonal. Heat the oil in a large frying pan, add the chorizo and fry for 3–4 minutes until golden brown, turning them over halfway. Remove and set aside.

Add the cachaça and let the alcohol bubble and burn off for 2 minutes, scraping the bottom of the pan. Add the onions and garlic and stir well. Fry for 2–3 minutes, until the garlic is fragrant and the onions are just beginning to soften but still have a little crunch to them. Return the chorizo to the pan and toss well to mix. If the mixture is too dry, add a tiny splash of water to the pan and stir. Transfer to a warmed serving dish and sprinkle with the chopped chives. Serve immediately.

CHICKEN ESPÍRITO SANTO
WITH TOMATO & PEANUT SAUCE

SERVES 4

Above the beaches of Rio lies the bohemian hillside village of Santa Teresa, where crumbling colonial architecture jostles for space with folksy craft shops, and the iconic yellow *bonde* tram shuffles its way up the cobbled streets. In amongst it is Espírito Santo, an Amazonian restaurant teeming with postcards of saints, indigenous headdresses and paintings by local artists. A dish of chicken skewers lightly rolled in chopped nuts was the stand-out dish on our visit, and our recipe is a tribute to this little neighbourhood restaurant. We've served it with our take on a typical Brasilian tomato and peanut sauce.

For the chicken skewers
60g brasil nuts
60g cashew nuts, lightly toasted
500g skinless, boneless chicken breasts or thighs
1 large egg
½ tsp sea salt
¼ tsp freshly ground black pepper
olive oil, to drizzle

For the tomato and peanut sauce
30g unsalted skinless peanuts
butter, for cooking
1 small onion, chopped
2 garlic cloves, chopped
¼ tsp ground coriander
2 tbsp tomato purée
2 plum tomatoes, deseeded and chopped
80ml coconut milk
½ tsp chicken bouillon or ½ stock cube
½ tsp caster sugar
sea salt and freshly ground black pepper

Preheat the oven to 180°C/350°F/Gas mark 4. Put the brasil nuts, cashew nuts and peanuts in separate corners of a baking tray and bake for 10–12 minutes, or until lightly toasted. Remove and leave to cool. Set the peanuts aside. Rub the brasil nuts with a kitchen towel to remove their skins, then place in a food processor along with the cashew nuts. Pulse the nuts to make coarse crumbs with a few larger chunks. Tip into a shallow bowl and set aside.

Next, make the tomato and peanut sauce. Melt the butter in a small saucepan and add the onion, garlic and ground coriander and season with salt and pepper. Cover and cook over a medium-low heat for 6–8 minutes, stirring occasionally, until soft and translucent. Add the rest of the ingredients and the

CONTINUED ⋙⟶

48

toasted peanuts and give the mixture a stir. Simmer for 8–10 minutes, or until the sauce has thickened. Transfer to a food processor and blend for about 1 minute. Taste and season with salt and pepper. Return to the pan and reheat before serving.

For the chicken skewers, preheat the oven to 180°C/350°F/Gas mark 4 and lightly oil a baking sheet. Slice the chicken into 2–3cm strips. Lightly beat the egg and season with salt and pepper. Coat the chicken strips in the egg, followed by the toasted nut crumbs. Thread the coated chicken on to metal skewers and place on the baking sheet. Drizzle with a little oil and bake for 12–15 minutes, until firm and just cooked through. Divide the skewers between warmed serving plates and serve with individual bowls of tomato and peanut sauce for dipping.

UPCYCLING

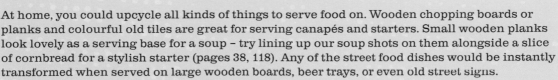

We've always been inspired by the Brasilian practice of 'upcycling': taking something old and recycling it into something that often turns out better and more beautiful than the original. We've seen everything, from children selling 'stolen' telephone wire woven into colourful bowls, to the work of Getúlio Damado, an artist who has been collecting rubbish and turning it into toys he's sold out of his wooden tram cart in the foothills of Santa Teresa for more than 40 years.

Back in London, we were delighted to discover Freddie Saul, who designed The Upcycled Furniture range with his father, the founder of fashion label Mulberry. Years ago, the EU banned the use of traditional wooden shelves for maturing cheese on health and safety grounds. Like Getúlio in Rio, Freddie saw the beauty of these ordinary objects, saved them from the scrap heap and turned them into beautiful tables, which inspired the tables in Cabana. If you look closely you'll see the ring marks left by the wheels of cheese.

At home, you could upcycle all kinds of things to serve food on. Wooden chopping boards or planks and colourful old tiles are great for serving canapés and starters. Small wooden planks look lovely as a serving base for a soup – try lining up our soup shots on them alongside a slice of cornbread for a stylish starter (pages 38, 118). Any of the street food dishes would be instantly transformed when served on large wooden boards, beer trays, or even old street signs.

GRILLED CRAB SHELLS

SERVES 4 AS A STARTER

In Brasil, you'll find the classic bar snack of grilled crab (*casquinha de siri*) served in scallop or crab shells – real or plastic – but you can just as easily use a ramekin. The *siri* crab is common in Brasil, but any fresh white crab meat can be used for our recipe.

It's best finished with a squeeze of lime to cut through the melted cheese and bring out the flavour of the crab. Serve with a side salad and an ice-cold beer as a summery starter.

300–400g fresh white crab meat (from an 800g–1.2kg cooked brown crab)
2 slices white bread, crusts removed
2 tbsp coconut milk mixed with 1 tbsp hot water
3 tbsp olive oil, plus extra for greasing
1 shallot, finely chopped
½ yellow pepper, deseeded and finely chopped
½ green pepper, deseeded and finely chopped
1 garlic clove, finely chopped
1 red chilli, deseeded and finely chopped
1 large plum tomato, deseeded and finely chopped
60ml white wine
15g desiccated coconut (or use freshly grated, if available)
1 tsp English mustard
juice of 1 lime, plus extra wedges to serve
small handful of coriander leaves, chopped
60g dried breadcrumbs
25g grated Parmesan cheese
20g cold butter
sea salt and freshly ground black pepper

Pick through the crabmeat to remove any bits of shell. Cover and place in the fridge. Tear the bread into small pieces. Put it in a bowl with the coconut milk and leave to soak for about 15 minutes.

Heat the oil in a large pan over a medium heat. Add the shallot, peppers, garlic, chilli and tomato and cook for 6–8 minutes, stirring occasionally, until softened. Add the wine and simmer until reduced by half. Stir in the soaked bread and desiccated coconut and cook for 1–2 minutes. Remove from the heat and stir in the crab meat, mustard, lime juice and coriander and season with salt and pepper. If it's too dry, add a little more coconut milk. Spoon into 4 lightly oiled ramekins or clean scallop shells.

Preheat the oven to 200°C/400°F/Gas mark 6. Mix the breadcrumbs and Parmesan and sprinkle them over the crab mixture. Cut the butter into very thin slices and place over the breadcrumbs. Bake for 10–12 minutes, until lightly golden brown. (If the topping isn't browning enough, put it under the grill for 2–4 minutes). Serve hot with wedges of lime.

The Brasilian love of grilled meat is legendary, and barbecue is at the heart of what we do at Cabana – particularly the foot-long metal skewers of fresh beef, pork, lamb or chicken, cooked to order on custom-made grills. They're inspired by Brasilian *churrascarias,* vast barbecue restaurants where you usually pay one price to eat as much meat as you can, and where you'll see everything from top cap of rump to chicken hearts.

Traditionally, meat is cooked very simply, but we have used typical Brasilian elements to create a wider range of flavours. Alongside the skewer recipes (which we have adapted for regular home grills), here's a selection of meat, fish and vegetables to slap on the coals when barbecue weather hits.

BRASILIAN
BARBECUE

SPICY MALAGUETA CHICKEN

SERVES 4

We knew from the very beginning that we wanted to create a dish using the *malagueta* chilli, a fiery Brasilian chilli similar to the Portuguese piri-piri. *Malagueta* chillies are ubiquitous in Brasil, and you'll find a bottle of them preserved in oil, vinegar or cachaça on every table top. After months of testing, we think we've got the right balance of sticky sweetness and chilli spice for the perfect marinade. The red peppers add extra sweetness and crunch. Leftover chicken can be used to spice up a salad, or you can use it in the Beirut (page 104) for a quick lunch.

500g boneless, skinless chicken thighs
5 tbsp Spicy Malagueta Marinade (page 88)
1 large red pepper
1 quantity Honey Mustard Glaze (page 89)
sea salt and freshly ground black pepper

Trim off any excess fat from the chicken thighs. Place them in a bowl, add the Spicy Malagueta Marinade and toss to coat evenly. Cover with clingfilm and store in the fridge. Let the chicken marinate for at least 4 hours, preferably overnight.

Light the barbecue and let the flames die down before starting to cook. If cooking indoors, preheat the grill to medium. Deseed the pepper and cut it into 2–3cm thick strips. Thread the peppers and chicken thighs alternately on to 4 or 5 metal skewers. Season with salt and pepper and cook for 10–15 minutes, turning occasionally. Baste with the honey glaze and return to the heat for a few more minutes until golden brown and just cooked through. The chicken thighs should feel firm when ready.

Remove the skewers and leave to rest for a few minutes, then serve hot. They're great with Sweet Potato Fries (page 120).

CABANA'S BARBECUING DO'S & DON'TS

DO

♥ Soak wooden skewers in cold water for at least 30 minutes before you use them, to prevent them scorching. If using metal skewers, wipe them with a piece of kitchen towel dipped in vegetable oil to stop food from sticking to them.

♥ Place bundles of fresh, hard-stemmed herbs and whole garlic cloves on the coals to add flavour to your food. Aromatic wood chips also work well.

♥ Make sure meat is cooked properly: check it is piping hot all the way through and that chicken or pork juices are running clear.

Leave time to get the meat up to room temperature before placing it on the grill. This will ensure that it cooks at an even rate.

♥ Be patient with charcoal. It takes 30 minutes to reach cooking temperature and should be white when you start to cook on it.

DON'T

✗ Leave meat in the middle of the barbecue for the entire cooking time. Place foods near the hot coals to sear the exterior at the beginning, then move further away to prevent the outside from burning before the inside is cooked.

✗ Leave all the preparation for your side dishes until you've started barbecuing, or you'll be faced with a mad rush.

✗ Poke the meat with anything sharp while it cooks, or the juices will escape; invest in a pair of tongs and put the meat on a side plate to check it.

✗ Let individual pieces of food touch on the grill. Keeping the meat separated will help it cook on all sides.

And finally,

✗ Be frustrated if the weather lets you down. Just heat up your grill oven, mix yourself a caipirinha and say *tudo bem*: everything's good.

CAIPIRINHA 'BEER CAN' CHICKEN

SERVES 4

In Brasil, roast chicken is sometimes known as 'television chicken' (*frango de televisão*) because the family dog can often be found with its head pressed to the oven, watching it cook. Our television chicken uses the flavours of a caipirinha and a can cooking method to create a succulent, sweet and sticky roast that can be cooked on the barbecue or in the oven. The can means that the chicken steams from the inside out, making the meat extra juicy and tender.

1 medium chicken (about 1.5–1.8kg)
olive oil, for drizzling
5 sage leaves, finely chopped
2 tbsp cachaça
1 tbsp soft brown sugar
sea salt and freshly ground black pepper

For the steam marinade
juice of 2 large limes
2 tbsp soft brown sugar
3 tbsp cachaça
3 garlic cloves, finely chopped or crushed
½ tsp sea salt
2 tbsp olive or rapeseed oil
5–6 large sage leaves, finely chopped

★ ★ ★ ★ ★ ★ ★ ★ ★ ★ ★ ★ ★ ★ ★ ★ ★ ★ ★

Light the barbecue (preferably one with a lid), and let the flames die down before starting to cook, or preheat the oven to 200°C/400°F/Gas mark 6. (If using charcoal, put most of the hot coals around the edges so there is indirect but even heat in the middle. If using a gas barbecue, set it to medium.)

Remove and discard the giblets and any excess fat in the cavity of the chicken. Rub it with a little olive oil, then rub it inside and outside with salt, pepper and chopped sage. Put all the ingredients for the steam marinade in a jug and stir to dissolve the sugar. Take an empty can and peel off any labels. Wash it out well, then pour in the marinade ingredients. Wrap the outside of a small heavy-based roasting tin with kitchen foil, then place the can in the middle. Sit the chicken on the can so that the top of it enters the cavity and the bird is upright. Spread out the legs to support the bird's weight. Take a squeezed lime half and pop it into the neck of the chicken to make a plug, or cover the neck cavity with foil to prevent the steam escaping while it cooks.

Roast for 45–55 minutes, until the chicken is almost cooked. Mix the remaining cachaça and sugar and carefully brush it over the chicken. Cook for 10–15 minutes, until golden and the juices run clear. Remove and let rest for 10–15 minutes. Carefully transfer to a serving plate, carve and serve it drizzled with the marinade, which will have reduced to a thick and tasty sauce.

ZINGY LIME & GARLIC CHICKEN

SERVES 4

As much as we love spice, we know not everyone likes a side of heat with their meal. This lime and garlic marinade results in tender, juicy chicken that's packed full of flavour, but without the chilli, therefore taking the heat down a notch.

500g skinless, boneless chicken thighs
6 tbsp Zingy Lime & Garlic Marinade
1 yellow pepper
1 quantity Honey Mustard Glaze (page 89)
sea salt and freshly ground black pepper
lime wedges, to serve

★ ★

Trim off any fat from the chicken thighs, then put them in a bowl. Add the marinade and toss to coat. Let the chicken marinate for at least 4 hours, or overnight.

Light the barbecue and let the flames die down before starting to cook. If cooking indoors, preheat the grill to high. Trim and remove the seeds from the yellow pepper and cut it into wedges. Thread alternating pepper strips and chicken thighs on to 4 or 5 metal skewers and season lightly with salt and pepper. Cook for 10–12 minutes, turning once or twice, until the chicken is almost cooked through.

Baste liberally with the honey mustard glaze, then return to the heat for another 2–3 minutes, until evenly golden brown. The chicken thighs should feel firm when ready.

Remove the skewers and leave to rest for a few minutes. Serve hot with lime wedges on the side. It's delicious with Biro-Biro Rice (page 114), Sweet Potato Fries (page 120) and Tomato & Palm Heart Salad (page 118).

ZINGY LIME & GARLIC MARINADE

MAKES ABOUT 350ML

This is a milder marinade we use for chicken. It's a good alternative for anyone who's not partial to chillies.

1 large onion, roughly chopped
5 large garlic cloves, roughly chopped
100ml lime juice
4 tbsp rapeseed or vegetable oil
4 tbsp mirin (Japanese sweetened rice wine)
40g flat-leaf parsley, roughly chopped
40g coriander, roughly chopped
1 tsp sea salt
1 tsp freshly ground black pepper

Put all the ingredients in a small food processor or blender and process until the herbs and garlic are finely chopped and you end up with a loose, wet paste. Use immediately or keep refrigerated in a clean sealed jar. It will keep well for a few days, although it may lose its vibrant green colour over time.

CACHAÇA GRILLED CHICKEN

SERVES 4

On a trip to Rio, David's old friend Miguel took us to his favourite *galetaria* (chicken shop), Sat's Galeto, and introduced us to a dish we instantly knew we wanted to include: chicken breast, flattened and butterflied, marinated in cachaça and oregano and lightly grilled. It's an original and crowd-pleasing addition to the barbecue.

500g boneless, skinless chicken thighs
3 garlic cloves, finely crushed
½ tsp dried or fresh chopped oregano
4 tbsp cachaça
2 tbsp olive oil
1 tsp sea salt
½ tsp freshly ground black pepper
few sprigs flat-leaf parsley, finely chopped
lime wedges, to serve (optional)

Open out the chicken thighs and place them on a chopping board. Cover them with clingfilm and lightly bash them with a meat mallet or rolling pin until the meat is of even thickness. Place in a shallow dish and add the garlic, oregano, cachaça, olive oil, salt and pepper. Use your hands to toss and coat the chicken, working the marinade into the flesh. Cover with clingfilm and chill for at least 4 hours.

Remove the chicken from the fridge half an hour before you start cooking and let it come to room temperature. Light the barbecue and let the flames die down before starting to cook. If cooking indoors, heat a griddle pan until hot. If you like, thread the chicken on to metal skewers, which will make it easier to turn them on the barbecue. Cook on the griddle or barbecue for 3–5 minutes on each side, until just cooked through – the chicken should feel firm when lightly pressed. Leave to rest for 5 minutes before serving with a sprinkling of chopped parsley and lime wedges on the side. We like to serve it with Grilled Portobello Mushrooms with Halloumi and Bahian-Spiced Aubergine (page 80).

BRASILIAN BEEF CUTS

There are several different types of restaurant in Brasil, all serving a range of cuts of meat. In *por kilo* restaurants, you pay for your food according to how much it weighs. *Churrascarias* are steak and barbecue houses; *rodizios* are restaurants in which waiters serve the food in a well-coordinated ballet of skewers. If you visit a *rodizio* or a *churrascaria*, the sheer number of cuts of beef can be overwhelming – the Brasilians take their meat very seriously. Normally they use only rock salt to bring out the flavour of the meat and lock in the moisture. At Cabana we tend to pare it down to the more familiar cuts and marinate them in a variety of sauces to add more complexity. We have a great appreciation for the variety of cuts available, though, and we're slowly introducing some of them in dishes such as the Picanha Burger (page 66), which makes use of Brasil's favourite cut of meat.

Here are five beef cuts you should definitely try if you're ever in Brasil.

 ## PICANHA

The cap of rump, the king of steaks in Brasil. A thick layer of fat, especially when the piece is folded on a skewer, adds to its distinctive flavour.

 ## CUPIM

A rich, fatty hump that needs to be slow-cooked to release its flavour. You need a cow with a hump, such as the Zebu, a variety that was introduced to Brasil from India over 100 years ago. *Cupim* means 'termite', probably because the hump looks like a termite mound.

 ## ALCATRA

The lean rump or top sirloin, from below the *picanha*.

 ## FRALDINHA

The flank or skirt may not seem like a choice cut, but it's extremely juicy and tasty. *Fraldinha* means 'little shirt-tail', or, less appealingly, 'nappy'.

 ## MAMINHA

The tri-tip, a triangular cut from the bottom of the sirloin, which is very lean, and perfect on a grill.

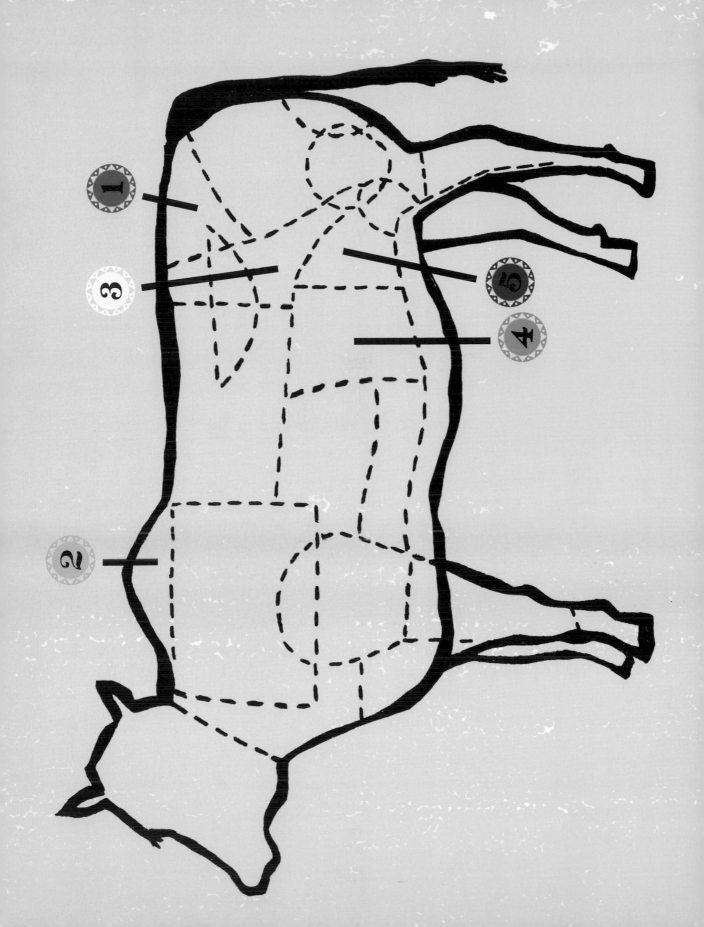

PICANHA BURGER

SERVES 4

This Anglo-Brasilian dish combines Brasil's favourite cut of meat with Britain's favourite barbecue dish. If you can't find *picanha* (cap of rump), or would prefer something lighter, you can substitute the same amount of good-quality minced beef. Potato matchsticks, or 'chipsticks', are popular in Brasil. You can find matchstick potatoes in larger supermarkets (they're sometimes called potato sticks or straw potatoes) or in specialist Latin American stores.

500g picanha, hand minced (or ask the butcher to mince it for you)
30g dried breadcrumbs
3–4 tbsp Chilli & Cumin Marinade (page 89)
olive oil, for brushing
4 brioche burger buns
4 tsp Chilli Mayonnaise (page 86)
3 plum tomatoes, sliced
4 tsp Chimichurri Marinade (page 88)
4–5 tbsp Black Beans (page 115)
handful of matchstick potatoes (optional)
sea salt and freshly ground black pepper

First, make the burgers. Put the beef mince and breadcrumbs in a large bowl, add the Chilli & Cumin Marinade, season with salt and pepper and mix well. Fry a teaspoon to taste it and check the seasoning; adjust if necessary. Divide the mince into 4 portions and moisten your hands. Shape each portion into a flat burger patty. Cover and chill the patties for at least 30 minutes to firm up.

Light the barbecue and let the flames die down before starting to cook. If cooking indoors, heat a griddle pan until very hot. If using a griddle pan, reduce the heat to medium, then lightly oil the patties and cook for 4–6 minutes on each side, until cooked to medium well. If using the barbecue, you may need to move them to a cooler section once browned. Remove and leave to rest for a few minutes.

Meanwhile, slice and toast the burger buns and warm up the black beans in a pan. To assemble, put the bottom halves of the buns on 4 serving plates, then spread the top halves with Chilli Mayonnaise. Arrange 3 tomato slices on each bun base and place a burger on top. Spoon over a little Chimichurri Marinade, followed by a tablespoon of black beans. Sprinkle the beans with potato matchsticks, if using, then add the burger bun tops. Serve immediately.

PORK WITH A PAR...ESAN CRUST

SERVES 4

Pork with Parmesan is a unique Brasilian dish that was probably created by Italian immigrants who took Parmesan to Brasil. Any tender cut of pork, such as fillet or loin, works well here: it's cooked, rolled in Parmesan and then grilled until the cheese forms a crispy crust. The Chimichurri Marinade is optional – if you don't have time to make it, the pork still tastes delicious with just the cheese crust.

500g pork fillet
juice of 1 lime, plus lime wedges to garnish
5 tbsp Chimichurri Marinade (page 88), or olive oil
75g Parmesan cheese, grated
sea salt and freshly ground black pepper
Molho Vinagrete (page 85), to serve

★ ★ ★ ★ ★ ★ ★ ★ ★ ★ ★ ★ ★ ★ ★ ★ ★ ★ ★

Trim the pork fillet of any fat or white membrane, then drizzle with the lime juice and Chimichurri Marinade, if using, and toss to ensure it is evenly coated, or simply rub with olive oil and season with salt and pepper. Cover and marinate in the fridge for 4 hours, or overnight.

Light the barbecue and let the flames die down before starting to cook. Cook the pork over direct heat on a barbecue for 2–3 minutes on each side, until evenly browned all over. Transfer to a cooler part of the barbecue, cover with a lid and continue to cook for about 10–15 minutes, until it is slightly springy to the touch or a pair of tongs. (Do check and turn the pork occasionally. Timings will vary depending on the thickness of the fillet and the intensity of the heat). Remove the pork and roll it in grated Parmesan until evenly coated. Cook for another 2–3 minutes, until the cheese has melted and is golden brown. The pork should feel just firm and the juices should run clear when you pierce it with a skewer. Rest for 5–10 minutes, then slice and serve with Molho Vinagrete. Delicious with Mango Salsa (page 86) and Grilled Pineapple (page 82).

VARIATION

Individual pork steaks can be cooked in the same way. Place 120–150g pork steaks between large sheets of baking parchment and bash until they are about 5mm thick. Coat with the lime juice and Chimichurri Marinade, if using, then cover and marinate in the fridge for 4 hours, or overnight.

Light the barbecue or preheat the grill to high and set the grill rack at the highest level. Scrape off any excess marinade and thread the pork on to metal skewers. Season lightly with salt and pepper (you'll be adding Parmesan later). Cook for 1½–2 minutes on each side. Remove and coat with Parmesan. Cook for 2–3 minutes, turning once, until the cheese is golden brown. Rest for 5 minutes before serving.

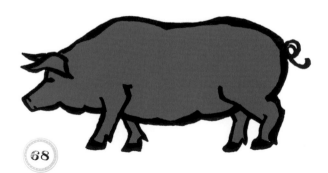

68

CHILLI & CUMIN MARINATED HANGER STEAK

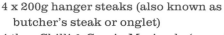

SERVES 4

At traditional Brasilian *churrascarias*, rock salt is usually sprinkled on the side of meat that faces the grill, then knocked off just before serving. It's tasty just like that, but we've adapted our steak to include a bit more spice. Our Chilli & Cumin Marinade is a blend of vinegar, cumin seeds, oregano and chilli flakes; we use it to marinate all our steaks, but it's equally good on lamb or fish.

4 x 200g hanger steaks (also known as
    butcher's steak or onglet)
4 tbsp Chilli & Cumin Marinade (page 89),
    plus extra for brushing
olive oil, for brushing
sea salt and freshly ground black pepper

★ ★ ★ ★ ★ ★ ★ ★ ★ ★ ★ ★ ★ ★ ★ ★ ★ ★ ★

Put the steaks in a large bowl and toss with the marinade. Cover with clingfilm and chill for at least 4 hours, or preferably overnight.

Half an hour before you are ready to cook, take the steaks out of the fridge and let them come to room temperature. Light the barbecue and let the flames die down before starting to cook. If cooking indoors, heat a griddle pan until very hot. Scrape the marinade off the steaks and pat dry with kitchen paper. Brush them with a little oil, season lightly with salt and pepper, then barbecue or griddle for 3–4 minutes on each side, or until cooked to medium rare. They should feel a little springy when pressed (see our handy guide on page 100). Remove from the heat and brush with a little marinade. Leave to rest for 5–10 minutes before serving. We like our steaks with Sweet Potato Fries (page 120) and a salad.

70

CHILLI & CUMIN MARINATED LAMB

SERVES 4

Beef is generally preferred over lamb in Brasil, but Chilli & Cumin Lamb has been one of the most popular dishes we've served at Cabana. We use lamb fillet because we think it's the most tender cut, but you could use diced leg or rump if you prefer. The palm hearts bring out the earthiness of the lamb.

600g lamb fillet
6 tbsp Chilli & Cumin Marinade (page 89)
400g tinned palm hearts, drained
sea salt and freshly ground black pepper

★ ★ ★ ★ ★ ★ ★ ★ ★ ★ ★ ★ ★ ★ ★ ★ ★ ★ ★ ★

Trim off any tough outer membranes from the lamb, then cut each fillet into evenly sized cubes, about 4cm each. Place in a bowl and toss with 4 tablespoons of the Chilli & Cumin Marinade. Cover with clingfilm and leave to marinate in the fridge for at least 4 hours, or preferably overnight.

Light the barbecue and let the flames die down before starting to cook. If cooking indoors, preheat the grill to medium and place the grill rack at the highest level. Cut each palm heart in half, then thread them on to metal skewers, alternating with the marinated lamb pieces. Season lightly with salt and pepper, then cook for 8–10 minutes, turning the skewers a few times, until evenly browned. The lamb is best cooked medium rare, and it should feel slightly springy when pressed.

Remove the skewers and brush with the remaining marinade. Rest for 5–10 minutes before serving. It works well with sides such as Broccoli Rice (page 116) and Black Beans (page 115).

GRILLED SEA BASS IN BANANA LEAVES

SERVES 4

Wrapping fish in banana leaves is popular in Brasil, where banana trees grow in abundance. Banana leaves are available in Asian or Latin American grocers, but you can substitute kitchen foil. You could also use other firm white fish such as sea bream, hake or whiting.

4 small whole sea bass (about 500–550g each), scaled and gutted
4 large banana leaves
4 limes, sliced
8 thick slices fresh root ginger
2 garlic cloves, thinly sliced
2 red chillies (preferably malagueta chillies), thinly sliced
large handful of mint leaves, roughly chopped

For the marinade
4 tbsp olive oil, plus extra for brushing
finely grated zest and juice of 1 lime
2 tsp soft brown sugar
sea salt and freshly ground black pepper

Light the barbecue, preferably one with a lid, and let the flames die down before starting to cook. Alternatively, preheat the oven to 200°C/400°F/Gas mark 6. Soak 8 wooden cocktail sticks for at least 20 minutes.

Rinse the sea bass and pat it dry with kitchen paper, then score the flesh on both sides. In a small bowl, combine all the ingredients for the marinade. Open the banana leaves and brush each one with a little olive oil. Place a sea bass in the middle of each leaf, then spoon over the marinade. Stuff the belly cavities of the fish with the sliced lime, ginger, garlic, chillies and mint leaves. Wrap the banana leaf around each one to form a loose parcel, then secure the ends with the cocktail sticks.

Place the parcels on the barbecue and close the lid, if you have one. Alternatively, cook on a baking tray in the oven. Cook for 20–25 minutes, depending on the size and thickness of the fish. Serve in the parcels. It's great with Grilled Pineapple (page 82), Mango Salsa (page 86) and Coconut Rice (page 114).

CHIMICHURRI MONKFISH

SERVES 4

Cooking fish on a barbecue can be tricky because it can easily flake and fall apart, but monkfish is firm enough to withstand the heat. You can use monkfish cheeks as we've done here, which are succulent and delicious, or ask your fishmonger for monkfish tails to grill whole and slice. The herby chimichurri marinade works brilliantly with it.

12 monkfish cheeks, about 500g in total (or use monkfish tails)
4 tbsp Chimichurri Marinade (page 88)
sea salt and freshly ground black pepper

Trim off any tough outer membrane from the monkfish, then put it in a bowl and toss with the marinade until evenly coated. Cover with clingfilm and chill for at least 4 hours.

Light the barbecue and let the flames die down before starting to cook. If cooking indoors, preheat the grill to high and place the grill rack at the highest level. Alternatively, you could also pan-fry the fish over a medium heat. Thread the monkfish on to 4 metal skewers and season lightly with salt and pepper. Barbecue or grill the skewers for 2–3 minutes on each side. The fish should be opaque and feel just firm when lightly pressed. Allow to rest for about 5 minutes before serving.

We like to serve the dish with Coconut or Biro-Biro Rice (page 114), Toasted Farofa (page 85) and Stir-fried Greens (page 115).

76

MALAGUETA JUMBO PRAWNS

SERVES 4

Prawns and barbecues are a match made in heaven: the tasty crustaceans are easy to grill, taste great with a slight char, and make an interesting alternative to the usual bacon and bangers. Try them with our Spicy Malagueta Marinade for an added kick.

12 large tiger prawns or 20 ordinary prawns
4 tbsp Spicy Malagueta Marinade (page 88)
sea salt and freshly ground black pepper
lime wedges, to serve

Peel and devein the prawns, but leave the tail ends on. Place them in a bowl and add 3 tablespoons Spicy Malagueta Marinade. Toss to coat, cover with clingfilm and leave to marinate in the fridge for a couple of hours.

Light the barbecue and let the flames die down before starting to cook. If cooking indoors, preheat the grill to high and place the grill rack at the highest level. Thread the prawns on to 4 metal skewers, then brush with the remaining marinade and season with salt and pepper. Barbecue or grill for about 2–3 minutes on each side, until they have turned opaque and are just cooked through. Serve with lime wedges on the side. They're delicious with Biro Biro or Coconut Rice (page 114) and a side salad.

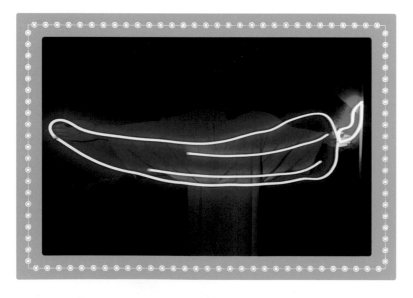

BRASILIAN BARBECUE

BAHIAN-SPICED AUBERGINE

SERVES 4–6 AS A SIDE DISH OR 2 AS A MAIN COURSE

Tempero baiano is a spice mixture from Bahia in eastern Brasil, which is often used to flavour fish, vegetables and soups. This is far more exciting than the usual vegetarian barbecue options, and can also be served as a side dish with barbecued meat.

1 large or 2 medium aubergines
olive oil, for brushing
2–3 tsp Chimichurri Marinade (page 88)
2–3 tsp Spicy Malagueta Marinade (page 88)
sea salt and freshly ground black pepper

For the tempero baiano seasoning
1 tsp cumin seeds
½ tsp dried parsley
½ tsp ground turmeric
½ tsp ground white peppercorns
¼ tsp cayenne pepper
1 tsp dried oregano

★ ★ ★ ★ ★ ★ ★ ★ ★ ★ ★ ★ ★ ★ ★ ★ ★ ★ ★

Light the barbecue and let the flames die down before starting to cook. If cooking indoors, heat a griddle pan until hot. Mix together all the spices for the seasoning and set aside. Cut the aubergine into 1.5cm thick slices. Brush the slices with olive oil, then sprinkle over the spice mixture and season lightly with salt and pepper. Thread the slices on to metal skewers.

Barbecue or griddle the aubergine slices for 2–4 minutes on each side, until tender and golden brown around the edges. Transfer to a serving plate, drizzle over a little of the Chimichurri and Spicy Malagueta marinades and serve warm.

GRILLED PORTOBELLO MUSHROOMS
WITH HALLOUMI

SERVES 4

On the beaches of Brasil you'll often come across men selling *queijo coalho*, a firm white cheese, grilled on skewers and often sprinkled with oregano and drizzled with molasses. Halloumi has the same squeaky texture and ability to withstand the heat of the barbecue. The cheese's saltiness works beautifully with the soft juiciness of the mushrooms.

★ ★ ★ ★ ★ ★ ★ ★ ★ ★ ★ ★ ★ ★ ★ ★ ★

8 large or 12 small Portobello mushrooms
3 garlic cloves, finely crushed
few sprigs thyme, leaves stripped
4 tbsp olive oil, plus extra to drizzle
250g halloumi cheese, sliced
small handful of flat-leaf parsley, finely chopped
sea salt and freshly ground black pepper

Light the barbecue, preferably one with a lid, and let the flames die down before starting to cook. If cooking indoors, preheat the grill to medium. Brush any dirt off the mushrooms and trim the stalks. Lightly oil a baking sheet and arrange the mushrooms on top, bottom-side up. Mix the garlic, thyme and oil in a small bowl, season with salt and pepper and spoon it over the mushrooms. Drizzle the edges with a little olive oil, then season with black pepper.

Cook the mushrooms over indirect heat on the barbecue or place the baking sheet under the hot grill for 7–8 minutes. When the mushrooms are cooked and tender, carefully place the halloumi slices on top. Return to the heat and cook for a couple more minutes, until the cheese has softened and is lightly golden around the edges. (If using the barbecue, you may need to cover it with a lid in order for the halloumi to melt and colour slightly.) Sprinkle with parsley and serve immediately, as the cheese will toughen as it cools.

GRILLED PINEAPPLE

SERVES 6–8

This dish can be sweet or savoury – it's up to you. The sweetness of the pineapple works well as a side dish with grilled meat or fish, or you can serve it with a scoop of ice cream or dollop of crème fraîche for an easy dessert.

1 medium pineapple
3 tbsp runny honey
juice of ½ lime
pinch of sea salt

★ ★

Cut the top and bottom off the pineapple, then stand it upright on a chopping board and slice off the skin all the way around. Remove any remaining eyes (the brown dots) with a small sharp knife. Turn the pineapple on its side and slice it into 1cm thick rounds. Use a small round pastry cutter to stamp out and discard the hard central core from each slice.

Light the barbecue and let the flames die down before starting to cook. If cooking indoors, lightly oil a griddle pan and heat until medium hot. In a small bowl, combine the honey, lime juice and salt to make a glaze. Brush the glaze over the pineapple slices, then barbecue or griddle them for 2–3 minutes on each side, or until caramelized around the edges. Turn the pineapple as it cooks, brushing it with a little more of the glaze. Drizzle the grilled pineapple with any leftover glaze and serve immediately.

GRILLED BANANAS & CHOCOLATE

SERVES 4

4 slightly under-ripe bananas
100g chocolate buttons
2 tsp ground cinnamon
4 tsp toasted desiccated coconut
vanilla or coconut ice cream, to serve (optional)

★ ★

When the barbecue coals are cooling down, this is a quick dessert to bang on the grill while you're enjoying your Spicy Malagueta Chicken. No, it's not strictly Brasilian, but bananas and chocolate are a classic combination, and it's the perfect end to a barbecue.

Allow the barbecue to cool a little or preheat the oven to 200°C/400°F/Gas mark 6. Peel the bananas, then cut a slit along the length of each one, taking care not to cut right through it. Place each banana on a large piece of kitchen foil, then stuff the slit with the chocolate buttons. Sprinkle a little cinnamon on top, then wrap the bananas to make individual parcels, crimping the edges of the foil to seal.

Place the parcels on the barbecue or cook on a baking tray in the oven for 5–10 minutes, until the chocolate has melted. Hand a banana parcel to each guest and serve with bowls of toasted coconut and ice cream.

SAUCES, DIPS & MARINADES

Here you'll find everything you need to dress up your dishes and give them that extra zing. As well as the marinades we use to enhance the flavour of our skewers, we've included sauces and dips that are as good with grilled meat as they are for accompanying our sides and street food, or for dressing salads. We've suggested some good combinations of sauces and main dishes, but feel free to play fast and loose with the rules and discover new combinations that suit your taste buds.

CABANA'S SIMPLE DRESSING

MAKES ABOUT 700ML

This is easy to make, and perfect for pepping up fresh green leaves.

3¼ tbsp Dijon mustard
4 tbsp tarragon vinegar
625ml extra-virgin olive oil
1 garlic clove, finely crushed
squeeze of lemon juice
½ tsp caster sugar, or to taste
¼ tsp sea salt, or to taste

Put the mustard and vinegar in a bowl and whisk well. Slowly whisk in the oil, ensuring the mixture emulsifies. Whisk in the rest of the ingredients and season with salt and pepper. Pour into a clean bottle or jar, seal and keep refrigerated. Use within a week or two.

MOLHO VINAGRETE

SERVES 4

Molho literally means 'sauce' in Portuguese, and *molho vinagrete* is a typical sauce used at Brasilian barbecues. The tangy flavours work well with most barbecue dishes.

3 ripe plum tomatoes (about 250g)
1 small onion
small handful of flat-leaf parsley
1 tbsp white wine vinegar
3 tbsp light olive oil
sea salt and freshly ground black pepper

Halve the tomatoes, scoop out the seeds with a teaspoon, chop them and place in a large bowl. Chop the onion to about the same size as the tomatoes and add to the bowl. Finely chop the parsley leaves and add them to the bowl.

Whisk the vinegar, oil and a pinch each of salt and pepper to make a dressing. Drizzle it over the tomato mixture and stir well. Spoon into one large or small individual bowls to serve.

TOASTED FAROFA

SERVES 4–6 AS AN ACCOMPANIMENT

Farofa is a flour made from ground cassava root. Toasted, it can be used to stuff chicken or fish, but is most often used as a side dish for grilled meats or stews to give them a savoury crunch. Meat eaters can fry 125g chopped smoky bacon until golden brown before adding the farofa. Cassava meal, known as *farinha de mandioca*, is available from specialist Latin American shops or online.

50g butter or olive oil
1 small red onion, finely chopped
1 garlic clove, finely chopped
200g cassava (manioc) meal

Melt the butter or oil in a frying pan over a medium heat. Add the onion and cook for 6–8 minutes, stirring frequently, until soft. Stir in the garlic and cook for 1 more minute, then add the cassava meal. Cook, stirring frequently, for 5–10 minutes, until it is lightly golden brown and resembles toasted breadcrumbs. It's best eaten immediately, but any leftovers can be reheated in a frying pan.

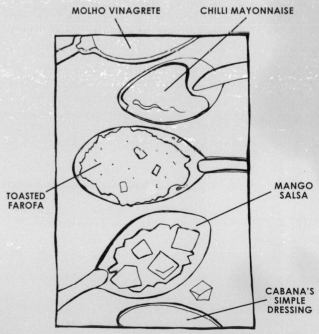

MOLHO VINAGRETE   CHILLI MAYONNAISE

TOASTED FAROFA

MANGO SALSA

CABANA'S SIMPLE DRESSING

KEY TO PICTURE ON PAGE 87

85

CHILLI MAYONNAISE

MAKES ABOUT 350ML

Slather this on our Picanha Burger (page 66), use it as a dip for Sweet Potato Fries (page 120), or serve it alongside street food snacks.

2 large egg yolks
1 tsp English mustard
1¼ tsp Dijon mustard
240ml rapeseed or vegetable oil
80ml light olive oil
1 tsp white wine vinegar (optional)
1¼ tsp lemon juice
½ tsp sea salt
2 tbsp tomato purée
1½ tbsp sweet chilli sauce, or to taste

Put the egg yolks and mustards in a small food processor and blend for a few minutes, until thick. Meanwhile, mix the rapeseed and olive oils together in a jug. With the motor running, slowly add the oil to the egg mixture in brief trickles, ensuring the mixture emulsifies. If it gets too stiff, add the vinegar to thin it down. If it curdles, pour it into a clean bowl, then add an egg yolk to the food processor and gradually whisk in the curdled mixture, followed by the rest of the oil.

Once about a third of the oil has been added, start drizzling in the rest in a steady stream, still blending. When all the oil has been incorporated, season with the lemon juice and salt. Finally, blend in the tomato purée and sweet chilli sauce. Keep refrigerated until ready to serve. It is best eaten within a week.

MANGO SALSA

SERVES 4

Mangoes grow in abundance in Brasil's tropical climate, in a rainbow of varieties. Juicy with mango flesh, tart and piquant with lime juice and chilli, this mango salsa is excellent with seafood, such as the Sweet Potato Crab Cakes (page 44), and also pairs nicely with grilled chicken and pork.

1 small ripe mango
1 red onion, finely chopped
2 spring onions, finely chopped
1 red or green chilli, deseeded and
   finely chopped
juice and zest of ½ lime
few sprigs of coriander, leaves chopped
sea salt and freshly ground black pepper

Peel the mango and cut off the flesh around the seed. Slice the flesh into 1cm dice and place in a large bowl. Add the rest of the ingredients, stir well and season with salt and pepper. Serve soon after preparing, as the coriander will darken once exposed to the lime juice.

SAUCES, DIPS & MARINADES

SPICY MALAGUETA MARINADE

MAKES ABOUT 275ML

This is Cabana's signature marinade and is used in our Spicy Malagueta Chicken and Jumbo Prawns (pages 54 and 78). The seeds are usually left in the chillies for heat, but you could remove them if you prefer a milder flavour.

70g small red chillies
    (preferably malagueta)
5 garlic cloves, lightly crushed
70ml light olive or sunflower oil
2 tbsp lemon juice
2½ tsp tomato purée
2½ tsp caster sugar
½ tsp dried chilli flakes
1 heaped tbsp sweet paprika
2 tsp sea salt
pinch of dried oregano

Preheat the oven to 180°C/350°F/Gas mark 4. Split the chillies lengthways and place them in a small roasting tray with the garlic and olive oil. Roast for 10 minutes. Leave to cool for a few minutes, then put the chillies, garlic and oil in a small food processor or blender and add the rest of the ingredients. Blend to a smooth purée. Transfer to a clean jar, seal and keep refrigerated for up to a week.

CHIMICHURRI MARINADE

MAKES ABOUT 175ML

Chimichurri is a fresh herb marinade that's Argentinian in origin, but has been adopted by Brasilian *churrascarias* (barbecue restaurants) as a marinade for steak and fish. It also works well with vegetables. We use it with Chimichurri Monkfish (page 76) and Grilled Portobello Mushrooms with Halloumi (page 80); you can also serve it as a dipping sauce with slices of fresh sourdough bread.

30g flat-leaf parsley
5 large garlic cloves
1 tsp dried oregano
150ml light olive or sunflower oil
½ tsp dried chilli flakes
35ml red wine vinegar
1 tsp sea salt
1 tsp freshly ground black pepper

Bring a small pan of water to the boil and have a bowl of iced water ready. Blanch the parsley for 1 minute, then drain it immediately and plunge it into the icy water. Drain and pat dry with kitchen paper.

Finely chop the parsley and garlic and place it in a bowl or a clean jar with lid. Add the rest of the ingredients and stir well. Alternatively, blend the blanched parsley with the rest of the ingredients in a food processor. Use immediately, or refrigerate in a sealed container and use within 3–4 days.

CHILLI & CUMIN MARINADE

MAKES ABOUT 175ML

This is a warming and subtly spiced marinade that we use for our Chilli & Cumin Marinated Hanger Steak, Lamb and Picanha Burger recipes (pages 70, 72 and 66).

70g red chillies (preferably malagueta), deseeded and roughly chopped
5–6 garlic cloves, roughly chopped
3 tbsp mirin (Japanese sweetened rice wine)
2 tbsp red wine vinegar
2 tsp sea salt
1 heaped tsp toasted cumin seeds
½ tsp dried oregano
60ml light olive or sunflower oil

Put all the ingredients in a small food processor and blend to a smooth, wet paste suitable for coating meats and fish. Use immediately or refrigerate for up to a week in a clean sealed jar.

HONEY MUSTARD GLAZE

MAKES ABOUT 50ML

This sticky glaze adds a great finishing touch to grilled meat and chicken.

2 tbsp honey
1 tbsp cider vinegar
1 tsp Dijon mustard

Stir all the ingredients together in a small bowl and use to brush over grilled meat to glaze it.

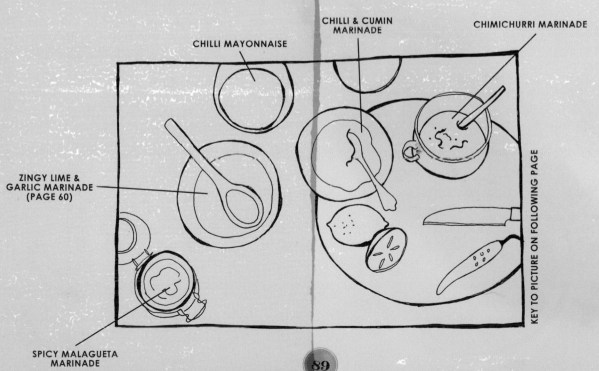

CHILLI MAYONNAISE

CHILLI & CUMIN MARINADE

CHIMICHURRI MARINADE

ZINGY LIME & GARLIC MARINADE (PAGE 60)

SPICY MALAGUETA MARINADE

KEY TO PICTURE ON FOLLOWING PAGE

BRASILIAN BARBECUE PARTY

Celebrate summer – and the Olympics in Rio – with this vibrant, simple and tasty plan-ahead barbecue menu. To serve 8–10 people, you'll need to double the quantities of the main course dishes you think will be the most popular, and also double up on the sauces, salads, grilled pineapple and Cabana Pimm's.

MENU

SPICY MALAGUETA CHICKEN
(PAGE 54)

CHIMICHURRI MONKFISH
(PAGE 76)

PORK WITH A PARMESAN CRUST
(PAGE 68)

GRILLED PORTOBELLO MUSHROOMS WITH HALLOUMI
(PAGE 80)

MOLHO VINAGRETE
(PAGE 85)

CORNBREAD
(PAGE 118)

FOUR-CORN SALAD
(PAGE 36)

TOMATO & PALM HEART SALAD
(PAGE 118)

GRILLED PINEAPPLE
(PAGE 82)

COCONUT & LIME SORBET
(PAGE 150)

CABANA PIMM'S
(PAGE 182)

SAUCES, DIPS & MARINADES

THE DAY BEFORE

- Make the Spicy Malagueta Marinade, put it on the chicken and marinate in the fridge overnight.

- Make the Cabana's Simple Dressing (page 85) for the salads and keep in the fridge.

- Make and freeze the Coconut & Lime Sorbet (one quantity will give one small scoop per person, which is fine as an accompaniment to the grilled pineapple, but double the quantities if you want to have plenty).

FOUR HOURS BEFORE GUESTS ARRIVE

- Make the Chimichurri Marinade, put it on the monkfish and refrigerate.

- Cut the large pineapple into rings and refrigerate. Prepare the glaze.

- Make the Molho Vinagrete.

- Prepare the portobello mushrooms for grilling.

- Prepare and bake the cornbread.

ONE HOUR BEFORE GUESTS ARRIVE

- Make both the salads but keep the dressing to one side for now.

- Thread the Spicy Malagueta Chicken onto the skewers.

TWENTY MINUTES BEFORE GUESTS ARRIVE

- Light the barbecue (see page 55).

- Grill the pineapple on the barbecue while the grates are still clean, then set aside.

- Make a large jug of Cabana Pimm's and chill it (don't add the ice just yet).

WHEN GUESTS ARRIVE

- Add the ice to the Cabana Pimm's and serve.

- Grill the Portobello Mushrooms and Chimichurri Monkfish.

- Dress the salads and slice the cornbread.

- Grill the Spicy Malagueta Chicken and Pork in a Parmesan Crust.

- Serve the grilled meats and fish with the sides and Molho Vinagrete.

- When ready for dessert, serve the Grilled Pineapple with Coconut & Lime Sorbet.

93

Cabana is inherently Brasilian, but we've absorbed other influences too. Paulistas (São Paulo natives) might be horrified that we marinate our meat in spices as well as brine, and Bahians might shudder to learn that we don't use *dende* (palm) oil in our coconut stews, but our dishes always remain true to what makes them essentially Brasilian: their origins and flavours.

Through our trips around the country, eating everywhere from market stalls, small *botecos* and traditional Bahian eateries to experimental modern restaurants, we've captured the essence of Brasilian dishes and given them our own twist to create updated versions of the classics. Jamie likes to call this 'new style': cooking that's Brasilian in spirit, but Cabana in creation.

NEW-STYLE BRASILIAN CLASSICS

PULLED PORK FEIJOADA

This is our new-style *feijoada* recipe, which combines black beans simmered with rich chorizo sausage and pulled pork. Our recipe is a quick and easy version of the traditional, rather complicated Brasilian stew – so you'll have more time to spend making caipirinhas!

FEIJOADA: THE SATURDAY MEAL

Although Sunday dinner is the big meal of the week in many parts of Europe, in Brasil it's all about Saturday lunch, when friends and family gather together to cook, eat, gossip and drink copious caipirinhas. It's integral to family life, a time to get together and catch up.

Central to the Saturday meal is Brasil's most iconic dish: *feijoada*. It's generally thought that it was invented by African slaves working on the plantations, who would save up the unwanted cuts of meat and cook them low and slow with beans, which were cheap and readily available. These days, though, there are many regional variations: pumpkin might be added in Bahia, white beans in the North East, or black turtle beans in Rio. In a traditional *feijoada completa*, the whole pig is used. You'll find dried beef, pork, cured meat and bacon along with pig's tongue, ear, foot and tail. If you go to a restaurant serving *feijoada completa* or visit a Brasilian friend on a Saturday, you'll find bowls of various stewed meats on the table alongside bowls of rice, farofa, collard greens and sliced oranges, so you can assemble a dish that's exactly to your liking. We've taken the essence of *feijoada* and used some of our favourite cuts of meat to make a classic, comforting dish that's easy to replicate at home.

1½ tbsp olive oil
3 cooking chorizo sausages, sliced
1 onion, chopped
1 stalk celery, chopped
1 carrot, chopped
4 garlic cloves, finely chopped
1 tbsp tomato purée
1 x 400g tin black turtle beans, drained
1 tbsp vegetable or chicken bouillon powder (or 1 stock cube)
few sprigs of thyme
225g Pulled Pork (page 32)
1 tbsp Spicy Malagueta Marinade (page 88)
small handful of flat-leaf parsley, finely chopped
sea salt and freshly ground black pepper

Heat the oil in a large pan and add the chorizo. Fry for 2 minutes on each side, until golden brown. Add the onion, celery, carrot and garlic and cook, stirring frequently, over a medium heat for 6–8 minutes, until softened. Stir in the tomato purée and season with salt and pepper. Fry for another 2 minutes, until the vegetables begin to colour.

Add the black beans and stir well. Add the stock powder and thyme leaves and stir again. If you find it a little too thick, add a splash of water – just enough to cover the ingredients. Part-cover the pan and simmer gently for 10–15 minutes, stirring occasionally, until everything is soft.

Add the Pulled Pork and Spicy Malagueta Marinade to the pan. Stir well, then taste and adjust the seasoning. Once the pork has heated through, stir in the chopped parsley and ladle into warmed bowls. Serve with Biro-Biro Rice (page 114), Toasted Farofa (page 85), orange wedges and potato matchsticks for the proper feijoada experience.

STEAK OSWALDO ARANHA

SERVES 4

Oswaldo Aranha was a Brasilian politician and diplomat who was fond of a restaurant called Cosmopolita in Rio. He was also a keen cook, and always asked for his steak with lots of fried garlic on top. Soon the waiters started referring to this as Steak Oswaldo Aranha, and it became a dish in its own right. You can use any type of steak, but we like the nice shape of rib-eye.

1 tbsp olive oil
2 tbsp butter
4 rib-eye steaks (about 225g each)
4 garlic cloves, thinly sliced
small handful of flat-leaf parsley, finely chopped
sea salt and freshly ground black pepper

★ ★ ★ ★ ★ ★ ★ ★ ★ ★ ★ ★ ★ ★ ★ ★ ★ ★ ★

Place a large heavy-based (preferably cast iron) frying pan over a high heat. Add the olive oil and 1 tablespoon butter and swirl the fats together as the butter melts. Season the steaks liberally with salt and pepper, then cook for 2–4 minutes on each side, depending on their thickness and how you like them cooked (see page 100). Try not to overcrowd the pan, or you'll end up stewing them. It's better to fry them in batches if your pan isn't wide enough. Remove the steaks and leave to rest for a few minutes.

Meanwhile, heat the remaining butter in another small pan and add the garlic slices. Fry over a medium-low heat until golden and crisp. Do not leave it unattended, as garlic can turn from golden to black in a matter of seconds. Once golden, tip the garlic and melted butter into a bowl.

To serve, place the steaks on warmed plates, then spoon over the crispy garlic slices and butter. Sprinkle over a little chopped parsley and serve immediately. We like them with Sweet Potato Fries (page 120) and Toasted Farofa (page 85).

THE FINGER TEST: HOW TO TELL WHEN YOUR STEAK IS DONE

Let's be honest, one of the biggest hassles of cooking steak is making sure that everyone gets their preference for how they like it cooked. Here's David's easy and foolproof method for testing the doneness of steaks, which should save time, money (no need to buy a meat thermometer) and the steak itself (no need to ruin it by making holes in it to check it).

To use this method, gently press your finger into the steak while it's cooking and compare it with the feel of your palm as described below. You'll be whipping up even the most complicated steak orders in no time!

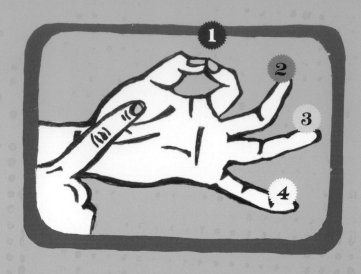

1 RARE

Lightly touch together the tips of your thumb and first (index) finger. Don't apply any pressure. Use your right index finger to press the fleshy area at the base of your thumb. This is how a rare steak should feel.

2 MEDIUM RARE

Next, lightly touch the tip of your thumb to your middle finger and feel the base of your thumb. This is medium rare.

3 MEDIUM

Then, lightly touch your thumb to your ring finger and feel the base of your thumb – this is what a medium steak feels like.

4 WELL DONE

Finally, lightly touch your thumb and little finger together and feel the base of your thumb. This is how a well-done steak will feel.

CHICKEN XIM-XIM

SERVES 6

Xim-Xim is another dish with African origins – in fact, the name comes from an African word for 'stew'. The traditional recipe calls for dried shrimp, which are popular in Brasil, but have a pungent flavour which isn't to everyone's liking, so we've substituted tomato paste to give a similar depth to the dish. Our version also includes basmati rice, resulting in a flavoursome, biryani-style one-pot meal. The pastry lid seals in the steam, which creates a moist, flavoursome dish.

600g boneless and skinless chicken thighs
3 garlic cloves, finely chopped
juice of 1 lime
1 tsp sea salt
1 tsp freshly ground black pepper
100g roasted unsalted cashews
100g roasted skinless and unsalted peanuts
4 tbsp olive oil
1 large onion, finely chopped
3cm piece fresh root ginger, peeled and finely grated
1–2 long red chillies, deseeded and finely chopped
1 tsp sweet paprika
pinch cayenne pepper
2 tbsp tomato purée
400g chopped tomatoes
2 tsp soft brown sugar
1 bouquet garni
200ml coconut milk
275ml chicken stock
200g basmati rice
200g Pastel dough (page 30), ready-made puff
    or shortcrust pastry
1 egg, lightly beaten

Cut the chicken thighs into bite-sized chunks and place in a bowl with the garlic and lime juice. Add ½ teaspoon each of salt and pepper, then cover in clingfilm and marinate for 30 minutes. Meanwhile, put the cashews and peanuts in a food processor and blend until they resemble coarse crumbs. Remove and set aside.

Preheat the oven to 200°C/400°F/Gas mark 6. Heat 2 tablespoons olive oil in a large pan, add the chicken pieces and cook for 2 minutes on each side, until lightly browned. Remove and set aside.

In the same pan, heat the remaining oil, add the onion and ginger and cook over a medium heat for 4–6 minutes, until softened. Add the chilli, paprika,

CONTINUED ≫≫→

NEW-STYLE BRASILIAN CLASSICS

cayenne pepper and tomato purée and fry for 1–2 minutes, then add the chopped tomatoes, sugar and bouquet garni and stir well. Simmer for 1 minute, then add the coconut milk and chicken stock. Season with the remaining salt and pepper, stir in the rice and return the chicken to the pan. Bring to the boil, then reduce the heat and simmer for 3 minutes, stirring occasionally to prevent it sticking. (The rice should be part-cooked at this point). Remove and discard the bouquet garni, then transfer to a large ovenproof dish. Leave to cool slightly.

Roll out the pastry thinly on a lightly floured surface to 3mm thick. (The pastry should be slightly wider than the diameter of the dish). Lightly brush the rim of the dish with the beaten egg, then drape the pastry over it. Press lightly to seal the overhanging crust to the sides of the dish. Brush the surface of the dough with beaten egg. Bake for about 30 minutes, then remove and let stand for 10–15 minutes before serving.

FITAS

In the city of Salvador, Bahia, lies one of Brasil's most famous places of worship: the Church of Nosso Senhor do Bonfim. It has a strong Catholic base but, like many of the churches in Salvador, it has incorporated a few elements of the traditional African faiths. It has become famous for its miraculous healing cures and is now a popular shrine. In the nineteenth century, Catholic pilgrims would arrive with pieces of silk tied around their wrists or necks with prayers or wishes written on them in ink. These days, people buy colourful replicas of these wish ribbons, known as *fitas*, which are stamped with the words *lembrança do senhor do bonfim da Bahia*, or 'souvenir of Our Lord of the Good End, in Bahia'. If you visit the Church, one of the first things you'll notice are the streams of *fitas* tied to the gates around the structure by pilgrims praying for good luck or for miraculous cures.

At Cabana, we give *fitas* out with our bills (and your bookmark is one), to spread a bit of good luck and wish you on your way. You tie it on your wrist with three knots and make a wish with each knot. When it falls off, throw it into running water and your wishes will come true.

Senhor do Bonfim bracelets may be hard to find unless you're visiting Brasil or Cabana (which, of course, we would highly recommend), but try giving out ribbons next time you have friends coming over, especially if you're going to be watching the football. Explain the legend, get everybody to make their wishes, and keep your fingers crossed. Good luck!

103

THE BEIRUT

SERVES 4

The Beirut was invented in the 1950s by two Syrian brothers who owned a diner in São Paulo. One day they ran out of regular sliced bread and served their native Syrian flatbread instead – and it was so popular they decided to keep it. The Beirut was born, and is still a favourite today, especially at Frevo diner in São Paulo, where we first tried it. Ours uses Spicy Malagueta Chicken (page 54; it's a good way to use up any leftovers), but you can substitute Zingy Lime and Garlic Chicken (page 60), or Portobello Mushrooms with Halloumi (page 80) as a vegetarian option.

4 large thick flatbreads
4 tbsp Chilli Mayonnaise (page 86)
70g wild rocket
3–4 plum tomatoes, sliced
600g cooked Spicy Malagueta Chicken (page 54)
50g Cheddar cheese, grated

★ ★ ★ ★ ★ ★ ★ ★ ★ ★ ★ ★ ★ ★ ★ ★ ★ ★ ★

Slice the flatbreads in half horizontally. Spread each bottom half with 1 tablespoon chilli mayonnaise, then add a handful of rocket leaves and arrange a layer of tomato slices on top. Slice the chicken into thin strips and arrange them over the tomatoes. Sprinkle over an even layer of cheese, then put the remaining flatbread halves on top.

Preheat a panini press or place a griddle pan over a medium-high heat. Cook for 3–5 minutes, until the flatbread is golden and the cheese begins to ooze out from around the sides. (If using a griddle pan, press down for 2 minutes while you cook each side). Remove and leave to cool while you cook the remaining sandwiches. Cut each one into quarters and serve warm.

NEW-STYLE BRASILIAN CLASSICS

BRASILIAN CHICKEN BUCKET

SERVES 4

This Brasilian-style fried chicken is the ultimate dish to enjoy with friends and the *futebol*. We've taken the traditional Brasilian fried chicken dish *franga passarinho* (which literally means 'chicken in the style of a little bird' because of the bite-sized pieces) and given it added crunch in the form of another well-loved Brasilian ingredient: matchstick potatoes. Best served with a beer in one hand and the remote control in the other.

450g skinless, boneless chicken thighs or breasts
2 garlic cloves, finely crushed
1 onion, finely chopped
2–3 tbsp cheiro verde (equal quantities of chopped flat-leaf parsley and spring onion)
5 tbsp lime juice
125g plain flour
1 tsp baking powder
2 tsp tempero baiano seasoning (page 80)
1 large (about 100g) baking potato
vegetable oil, for deep frying
sprig of flat-leaf parsley, finely chopped
Chilli Mayonnaise, to serve (page 86)
sea salt and freshly ground black pepper

★ ★ ★ ★ ★ ★ ★ ★ ★ ★ ★ ★ ★ ★ ★ ★ ★ ★ ★ ★

Cut the chicken into 3cm pieces, then place in a large bowl. Add the garlic, onion, cheiro verde and lime juice, and season with salt and pepper. Toss to coat and leave to marinate for 20–30 minutes (or cover and chill for a couple of hours).

Put the flour, baking powder and tempero baiano seasoning in a large bowl and mix well. Peel the potato, then finely grate it over the bowl using a mandolin. The pieces should be as fine as matchsticks. Mix the potatoes with the flour until evenly coated.

Heat the oil in a deep-fat fryer to about 180°C/350°F. Add the potato and flour mixture to the bowl of marinated chicken and mix well. Fry the chicken in batches, making sure each piece is well coated with the potato matchsticks and batter. Fry each batch for 2–3 minutes, then turn it over and cook until both sides are evenly browned and crisp. Remove and drain on kitchen paper. Keep warm while frying the remaining chicken. Sprinkle with parsley and salt and serve hot, with Chilli Mayonnaise on the side.

NEW-STYLE BRASILIAN CLASSICS

LOBSTER & PRAWN MOQUECA

SERVES 4

Moqueca ('mo-keh-ka') is a coconut seafood dish from Bahia in tropical eastern Brasil. The name comes from an African word for fish stew, and white fish is often used, but for our version we've chosen juicy prawns and lobster, inspired by a trip to Siri Mole restaurant in Rio.

1 tbsp olive oil
2 tbsp palm oil, or more olive oil
1 onion, finely chopped
1 small red pepper, deseeded and finely diced
1 small green pepper, deseeded and finely diced
3 garlic cloves, finely chopped
2 plum tomatoes, deseeded and finely diced
2 heaped tbsp tomato purée
400ml coconut milk
350g raw prawns, shelled and deveined
250g cooked lobster tail (or flesh from 1 whole cooked lobster), cut into bite-sized pieces
juice of ½ lime, plus extra wedges to serve
small handful of coriander, chopped
sea salt and freshly ground black pepper
lime wedges, to serve

★ ★ ★ ★ ★ ★ ★ ★ ★ ★ ★ ★ ★ ★ ★ ★ ★ ★

Heat the oils in a large heavy-based pan, add the onion, peppers and garlic and season with salt and pepper. Stir well and cook gently for 6–8 minutes, stirring, until softened. Stir in the diced tomatoes and tomato purée and cook for 2 more minutes. Pour in the coconut milk and bring to the boil. Reduce the heat and simmer for about 5 minutes. Add the prawns and cook gently for 3–4 minutes, until they have just turned opaque. Add the lobster and cook for another 2 minutes. Turn off the heat, add the lime juice and coriander, then taste and adjust the seasoning. Ladle into individual warmed bowls and serve with lime wedges. Coconut or Biro-Biro Rice (page 114) and Toasted Farofa (page 85) are great with it.

VEGETABLE MOQUECA

SERVES 4–6

We were interested to find this vegetarian version of *moqueca* on the menu in a Bahian restaurant in Rio. It reflects a gradual change in the country's diet, and the increasing popularity of vegetarian versions of classic dishes.

2 tbsp olive or palm oil
1 white onion, chopped
1 green pepper, deseeded and thinly sliced
1 red pepper, deseeded and thinly sliced
4 spring onions, trimmed and finely chopped
3 garlic cloves, finely chopped
2 tsp sweet paprika
½–1 tsp chilli powder (to taste)
400ml coconut milk
100ml vegetable stock
2 large tomatoes, deseeded and chopped
2 tbsp tomato purée
1 aubergine, cut into 2.5cm chunks
2 large or 3 small courgettes, cut into 1.5cm chunks
juice of 1 lime
handful of coriander, roughly chopped
sea salt and freshly ground black pepper

★ ★ ★ ★ ★ ★ ★ ★ ★ ★ ★ ★ ★ ★ ★ ★ ★

Heat the oil in a large pan over a medium heat and fry the onion and peppers for 4–6 minutes, until softened. Add the spring onions, garlic, paprika and chilli powder and cook for another minute. Add the coconut milk, vegetable stock, chopped tomato and tomato purée, bring to a simmer and cook, uncovered, for 5 minutes. Season with salt and pepper.

Add the aubergines and cook for 2 minutes before adding the courgettes. Simmer for another 3–4 minutes, until the vegetables are just tender, but not overcooked and mushy. Add the lime juice, then taste and adjust the seasoning. Take the pan off the heat and add the coriander. Serve in warmed bowls, with Coconut or Biro-Biro Rice (page 114) and Toasted Farofa (page 85) on the side.

PRAWNS IN A PUMPKIN

SERVES 4

This is a fantastic, crowd-pleasing dish from northeastern Brasil. The prawns are cooked in a light curry sauce, then served inside a baked whole pumpkin or round squash (such as kabocha) for people to help themselves. It's a hearty autumnal dish that would make an impressive main course for a Halloween party served with a side of Coconut Rice (page 114) or Cornbread (page 118).

1 medium pumpkin or 4 small round squash
500g raw prawns, peeled and deveined
juice of 1 lime
½ small red chilli, deseeded and finely chopped
2 bay leaves
4 tbsp olive oil
butter, for cooking
1 onion, finely chopped
2 garlic cloves, finely chopped
4 tomatoes, peeled, deseeded and chopped
100ml white wine
½–1 tbsp curry powder (or to taste)
2½ tbsp plain flour
150ml vegetable stock
1–2 tbsp finely chopped flat-leaf parsley
sea salt and freshly ground black pepper

★ ★ ★ ★ ★ ★ ★ ★ ★ ★ ★ ★ ★ ★ ★ ★ ★ ★ ★

Preheat the oven to 200°C/400°F/Gas mark 6. Cut out a lid from the pumpkin (as if you were carving a jack-o'-lantern) and scoop out all the seeds and strings. Wash it inside and out and pat dry with kitchen paper. Replace the lid. Wrap in kitchen foil and roast for 1 hour, or until tender.

Meanwhile, combine the prawns with the lime juice, chilli, bay leaves and 2 tablespoons olive oil and season with salt and pepper. Mix well and leave to marinate for 10–15 minutes. Heat the remaining olive oil and a little butter in a large frying pan, add the onion and cook gently for 4–5 minutes, stirring, until translucent. Add the garlic and cook for 30 seconds. Stir in the tomatoes and cook for 5 minutes, stirring. Add the wine and boil until reduced by half. Add the curry powder and flour to the pan and stir well. Cook for a few minutes before adding the stock, then simmer gently for about 10 minutes.

While the sauce is cooking, heat a large frying pan until hot. Fry the prawns in batches (avoid overcrowding the pan) until they have turned pink and opaque. Add the cooked prawns to the tomato sauce. When the pumpkin is ready, remove the lid and leave the bottom covered in foil. Ladle the prawns into the pumpkin and bake for 10 minutes more. Remove the foil and place in a serving dish. Sprinkle with chopped parsley and serve with a ladle for guests to help themselves.

Rice and beans are such a staple part of Brasilian cuisine that the traditional saying *o arroz com feijão* ('the rice and beans') means 'the basics' or 'the heart of things'. Beans, soaked overnight and cooked low and slow for hours, are served alongside fluffy long-grain white rice as a perfect accompaniment to simply but elegantly cooked meat or fish.

As well as these key dishes, here's a selection of our favourite Brasilian side dishes, including regional specialities like the tropical sweetness of Bahian Coconut Rice and a hearty bowl of Stir-Fried Greens from Minas Gerais.

SIDES & SALADS

BIRO-BIRO RICE
SERVES 4

Antônio José da Silva Filho, better known as Biro-Biro, is a retired Brasilian footballer. It seems he loved this dish of stir-fried rice topped with crispy onions so much that the Brasilians named it after him. It can be served alongside most dishes, from Pulled Pork Feijoada (page 96) to Spicy Malagueta Chicken (page 54). Any leftovers can be used to make crunchy rice Bolinhos (page 31).

For the crispy shallots
vegetable or groundnut oil, for deep-frying
¾ tsp sea salt
75g plain flour
1 banana shallot, sliced into thin half-moons
100ml milk

For the rice
200g basmati rice
3 tbsp olive oil
1 red onion, finely chopped
4 spring onions, chopped
small handful of flat-leaf parsley, chopped
sea salt and freshly ground black pepper

★ ★ ★ ★ ★ ★ ★ ★ ★ ★ ★ ★ ★ ★ ★ ★ ★

First, make the crispy shallots. Heat the oil in a deep-fat fryer to 190°C/375°F. Mix the salt with the flour and coat the shallot slices with it: put it all in a small plastic bag, hold tightly and shake well, then tip out into a sieve and shake off any excess. Dip the coated slices in milk, drain, then coat again with the flour. Shake off any excess. Fry in batches until golden brown, then remove and drain on kitchen paper. Sprinkle with salt while hot.

Wash the rice in cold running water. Drain, put in a small saucepan with 350ml water and bring to the boil. Reduce the heat to a simmer, cover and cook for 10 minutes, until it has absorbed most of the water. Remove from the heat and leave to steam, covered, for 10 minutes.

Heat the oil in a large pan, add the red onions and season with salt. Fry over a medium heat for 6–8 minutes, until softened. Add the rice and stir well. Stir in the spring onions and parsley. Season with salt and pepper. Serve warm, topped with the crispy shallots.

COCONUT RICE
SERVES 4–6

Coconut rice is popular in Bahia, and is a perfect accompaniment to seafood dishes like our Lobster & Prawn Moqueca (page 108) or Grilled Sea Bass in Banana Leaves (page 76). Bahian cuisine is the spiciest food in Brasil, so the sweetness and richness of this side works well with dishes from this region, or with curries or spicy dishes from other parts of the world.

250g basmati or long-grain rice
1 tbsp olive oil
1 onion, finely chopped
1 tsp caster sugar
1½ tsp sea salt
50g grated fresh coconut (optional)
200ml coconut milk
50g coconut flakes, to serve
few sprigs of coriander, to serve

Put the rice in a sieve and wash under cold running water until the water runs clear. Leave to drain for a few minutes.

Heat the oil in a saucepan over a medium heat. Add the onion and cook gently for 6–8 minutes, until softened. Add the sugar, salt and rice and cook for another minute. Stir in the grated coconut now, if using. Pour in the coconut milk and 200ml water and stir again. Bring to the boil, reduce the heat to low and cover the pan. Simmer for 10 minutes, until most of the liquid has been absorbed. Remove from the heat and leave to steam, covered, for 10 minutes.

Meanwhile, toast the coconut flakes in a dry frying pan over a medium-high heat. Stir or toss the coconut flakes occasionally to toast them evenly. Do not leave the pan unattended, as they burn easily. When lightly golden and fragrant, tip into a bowl and leave to cool slightly.

Flake the cooked coconut rice with a fork and spoon into warmed serving bowls. Garnish with coriander and toasted coconut flakes and serve hot.

BLACK BEANS

SERVES 4

Brasilians love black beans (*feijão*) so much that apparently, during World War II when fuel was rationed, savvy housewives would dig an outdoor cooking pit to cook them very slowly, using as little fuel as possible. Some would even drop a washed can of condensed milk into the bean pot to make Doce de Leite (page 144) at the same time. The traditional recipe uses dried beans, which involves soaking them overnight and using a pressure cooker, but use tinned beans to save time. You could add bacon lardons to the pot if you'd like a meatier flavour.

2 tbsp olive oil
1 large onion, finely chopped
1 garlic clove, finely chopped
1 small carrot, finely diced
1 celery stick, finely diced
½ tsp ground cumin
½ tsp paprika
1½ tbsp tomato purée
2 x 400g tins black beans in water
1 heaped tsp vegetable bouillon powder
    (or 1 vegetable stock cube)
few sprigs of thyme, leaves stripped
200g lardons (optional)
sea salt and freshly ground black pepper

Heat the oil in a large saucepan, add the chopped vegetables and cook over a medium-low heat, stirring occasionally, for 8–10 minutes, until softened. Stir in the spices and cook for a further 2–3 minutes until they release their fragrance. Add the tomato purée, the black beans and their liquid, the vegetable bouillon and thyme and give it a good stir. Simmer for 10–12 minutes to reduce some of the liquid.

If using lardons, heat a little olive oil in a large saucepan over a medium heat, add the lardons and cook for 5–10 minutes until the fat has rendered out and they are crispy and brown. Add to the beans just before serving.

Taste and season with salt and pepper. Serve in warmed bowls.

STIR-FRIED GREENS WITH GARLIC

SERVES 4

There's an old wives' tale in Brasil that a woman was only ready for marriage if she knew how to kill, pluck and cook a chicken and finely slice a bunch of collard greens. Stir-fried collard greens, or *couve* ('ku-veh') as they are called in Brasil, is a dish from the Minas Gerais region and is a popular accompaniment to Feijoada (page 96) or as part of the *prato executivo* (businessman's lunch).

400g seasonal greens (such as mustard
    greens, Swiss chard, sweetheart cabbage,
    spinach or young kale)
2 tbsp olive oil
3 large garlic cloves, finely chopped
butter, for cooking
sea salt and freshly ground black pepper

Wash the greens well, then remove any tough stalks and chop or shred the leaves (extra finely, if your future mother-in-law is watching).

Heat the oil in a large pan or wok over a medium heat. Add the garlic and let it gently infuse with the oil for a few minutes, without allowing it to burn. When you begin to smell the aroma of the garlic, and before it begins to colour, add the greens a handful at a time, stirring well each time. Season with salt and pepper and add a tiny splash of water. Stir well and cover with a lid. Cook until just tender (cooking time will vary from 2–10 minutes, depending on the type of greens, so taste a little every few minutes to check). Stir in the butter and check the seasoning. Transfer to warmed bowls and serve immediately.

BROCCOLI RICE

SERVES 4–6

Broccoli rice is popular at buffets and parties, even if broccoli itself isn't seen that often. We tried it at Sat's Galeto in Rio and loved the garlicky flavour and vibrant green flecks the broccoli gives the rice. For our own (optional) variation, we sometimes add creamed spinach, which gives a richer flavour and a more intense green colour.

1 head broccoli
3 tbsp olive oil
1 small onion, finely chopped
2 garlic cloves, finely chopped
¾–1 tsp garlic salt, to taste
300g cooked basmati or long-grain rice
freshly ground black pepper

★ ★ ★ ★ ★ ★ ★ ★ ★ ★ ★ ★ ★ ★ ★ ★ ★ ★ ★

Remove the broccoli stalk and save it for another dish. Finely chop the broccoli florets. Heat the olive oil in a large shallow pan, preferably non-stick. Add the onion and cook gently for 6–8 minutes, until soft and translucent but not coloured. Add the garlic and cook for 1 more minute, until fragrant. Stir in the broccoli and garlic salt. Add a small splash of water and cook for 2–3 minutes, until the broccoli is tender and a vibrant green colour. Add the rice and stir well, breaking up any large lumps. Continue to stir-fry for a few more minutes until the rice is hot. Season with black pepper and more salt if needed. Spoon into warmed bowls and serve immediately.

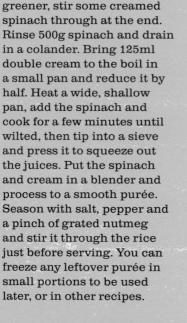

VARIATION

To make the rice even greener, stir some creamed spinach through at the end. Rinse 500g spinach and drain in a colander. Bring 125ml double cream to the boil in a small pan and reduce it by half. Heat a wide, shallow pan, add the spinach and cook for a few minutes until wilted, then tip into a sieve and press it to squeeze out the juices. Put the spinach and cream in a blender and process to a smooth purée. Season with salt, pepper and a pinch of grated nutmeg and stir it through the rice just before serving. You can freeze any leftover purée in small portions to be used later, or in other recipes.

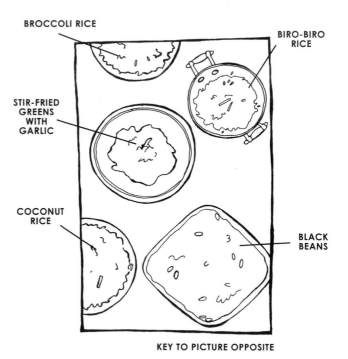

BROCCOLI RICE

BIRO-BIRO RICE

STIR-FRIED GREENS WITH GARLIC

COCONUT RICE

BLACK BEANS

KEY TO PICTURE OPPOSITE

116

TOMATO & PALM HEART SALAD

SERVES 4

Palm trees grow in abundance in Brasil, so it's no wonder that palm heart (*palmito*, or the more sustainable *pupunha* variety) is a staple of the cuisine, either roasted, grilled in roundels or eaten fresh, tossed in a salad like this one. The salad works perfectly with barbecue dishes or as a light side dish with Caipirinha 'Beer Can' Chicken (page 58).

4 ripe plum tomatoes
400g tin or jar palm hearts, drained
about 100ml Cabana's Simple Dressing
   (page 85)

Cut the tomatoes into wedges and place in a bowl. Slice the palm hearts and add to the bowl. Drizzle over enough dressing to coat and give the salad a gentle toss. Divide among individual bowls to serve.

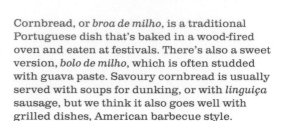

CORNBREAD

SERVES 8

Cornbread, or *broa de milho*, is a traditional Portuguese dish that's baked in a wood-fired oven and eaten at festivals. There's also a sweet version, *bolo de milho*, which is often studded with guava paste. Savoury cornbread is usually served with soups for dunking, or with *linguiça* sausage, but we think it also goes well with grilled dishes, American barbecue style.

100g fine cornmeal or polenta
100g plain flour
¾ tsp sea salt
1 tbsp baking powder
½ tsp baking soda
75g caster sugar
2 large eggs
150ml buttermilk
4 tbsp olive oil, plus extra for greasing
200g creamed sweetcorn

Preheat the oven to 180°C/350°F/Gas mark 4. Lightly grease a 20cm square baking tin with olive oil and line the base with baking parchment.

Sift all the dry ingredients into a large bowl. Beat the eggs, buttermilk and oil together in a separate bowl. Pour the egg mixture into the dry ingredients and fold it through. Finally, fold in the creamed sweetcorn, then pour into the prepared tin and spread out evenly.

Bake for 20–25 minutes, until it is golden brown and a skewer inserted in the middle of the cornbread comes out clean. Remove and leave to cool slightly. Cut into 16 squares and serve warm.

FRIED BANANAS

SERVES 4-6

Fried bananas are often served in Brasil as an accompaniment to grilled meat – try them with Steak Oswaldo Aranha (page 98) or Chilli & Cumin Marinated Hanger Steak (page 70). Traditionally, a semi-sweet banana variety such as *banana prata* (silver banana) is used, but you can substitute slightly under-ripe bananas, or even plantains.

60g plain flour
2 eggs
50g fresh breadcrumbs
50g panko breadcrumbs
4–6 firm, slightly under-ripe bananas
vegetable or groundnut oil, for frying
sea salt

Mix the flour with a pinch of salt in a shallow bowl. Lightly beat the eggs in a separate bowl and mix together the two types of breadcrumbs in a third bowl.

Peel the bananas and halve them lengthways. Coat the banana halves evenly with the seasoned flour, egg and breadcrumbs. Set aside.

Heat enough oil to shallow fry the bananas in a wide, shallow pan. (If using a deep-fat fryer, heat the oil to 180°C/350°F). When the oil is hot, add the bananas in batches and cook for about 2 minutes on each side, until golden brown. Remove and drain on kitchen paper. Transfer to a warmed plate and serve immediately.

SWEET POTATO FRIES

SERVES 4

These fries are one of the most popular dishes at Cabana. The sweet potatoes turn a wonderful bright orange when fried, and are complemented by the deep red paprika, which adds a subtle spice.

500g (about 2 large) sweet potatoes
vegetable oil, for deep-fat frying
1 tsp smoked paprika
sea salt

Cut the potatoes lengthways into 1cm thick chips. Heat the oil in a medium pan or deep-fat fryer to 130°C/265°F. Fry the potatoes in small batches for 3–4 minutes, until soft and tender but not browned. Remove and drain on kitchen paper. Set aside at room temperature.

When you are ready to eat, heat the oil to 180°C/350°F. Carefully add a batch of par-cooked chips to the hot oil and cook for 2–4 minutes, until golden brown and crisp. If not using a deep-fat fryer, you may need to adjust the heat if the chips brown too quickly. Remove and drain on kitchen paper. While hot, sprinkle with a little smoked paprika and sea salt. Keep warm while frying the rest of the chips. Transfer to 1 large or individual warmed bowls and serve immediately.

AVOCADO & MANGO SALAD

SERVES 4

Avocados are considered a fruit in Brasil (which they are, botanically speaking), and are therefore usually eaten sweet as a dessert. Savoury uses are gradually starting to become more popular, though. Make sure you use ripe avocados for this – to check, flick the stem; if it falls off easily and is green underneath, you know it's ready to use; if it's stuck fast, it's not ripe; if it's brown underneath, it's over-ripe.

1 small head round lettuce
70g watercress
1 small ripe mango
1 ripe avocado
1 small red chilli, deseeded and finely chopped
about 100ml Cabana's Simple Dressing (page 85)

Trim the base of the lettuce and tear the large outer leaves into smaller pieces. Pick the leaves off the watercress stems. Peel the mango and slice the flesh around the seed into thin strips. Halve the avocado and remove the stone, then peel off the skin and roughly chop the flesh or cut it into strips.

To assemble the salad, divide the lettuce leaves between 4 bowls, then top with the watercress, mango and avocado. Add the chilli to the dressing and drizzle 1–2 tablespoons of it over the salad when ready to serve.

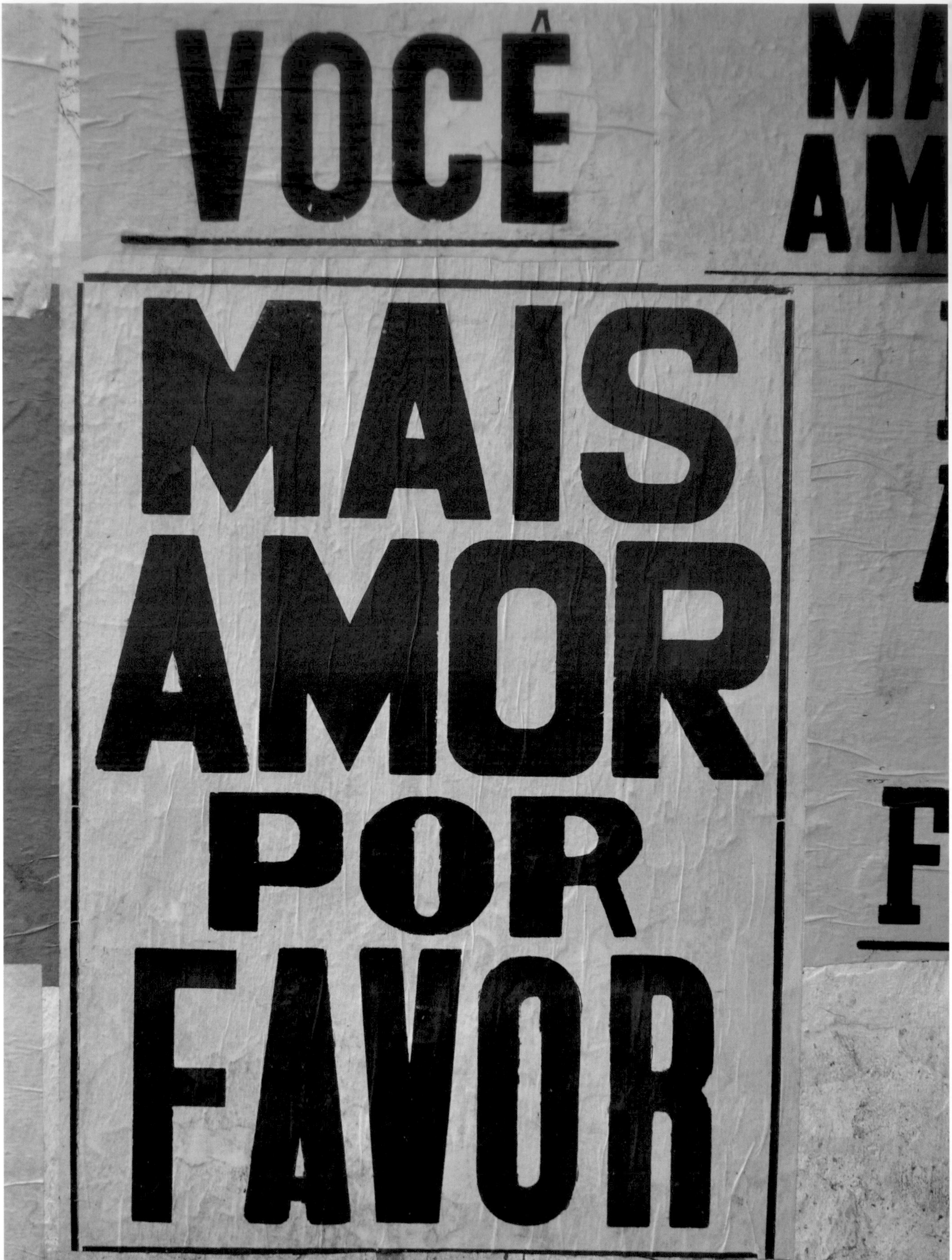
VOCÊ
MAIS AMOR POR FAVOR

LAMBE-LAMBE

At Cabana, the walls are covered floor to ceiling in *lambe-lambe* posters. Literally meaning 'lick-it lick-it', *lambe-lambe* is a style of fly-posting once popular in São Paulo before it was banned as part of the masterplan to clean up the city.

We came to *lambe-lambe* in a roundabout way. We knew the graffiti work of the art collective Choque Cultural, and when we were first researching the architecture and interior design for the restaurants we visited their São Paulo gallery. We wandered down a tiny staircase and discovered a basement completely wallpapered in *lambe-lambe*. They put us in touch with their printers, and we arranged to meet in their tiny hut in the suburbs. It was a revelation.

Mauricio and Carlos, the octogenarian duo behind Grafica Fidalga, print using their 1929 German letterpress, which was originally imported to help produce the weekly newspaper of the Socialist Workers' Party, and later used to make posters to advertise the Carnaval and other music events. The letters and symbols are hand made in eucalyptus wood and last for up to 15 years. When *lambe-lambe* was banned, Mauricio and Carlos became artists, highly sought after for their skill and design. This seemed to us to represent the best of Brasilian creativity: something unique and inspirational coming out of adversity.

We told them vaguely what we were after and spent a whole day watching as they typeset and danced the samba. Then, armed with hundreds of posters, we headed back to England, where their unique artwork has gained a new audience.

PRAWN, PINEAPPLE & PALM HEART SALAD
WITH HONEY–CINNAMON DRESSING

SERVES 4

This recipe is inspired by a dish we had at Dalva e Dito restaurant in São Paulo. In our version, hearts of palm are tossed with grilled prawns and sweet pineapple chunks, then drizzled with a honey-cinnamon dressing. It can be served as a side or is great on its own as a light main course. If serving as part of a barbecue, use freshly grilled prawns to give it a slightly smoky dimension.

350g (1 small) ripe pineapple, diced
250g cooked king prawns
1 x 400g tin palm hearts, drained and thinly sliced
small handful of mint, leaves chopped
small handful of flat-leaf parsley, leaves chopped
large handful of rocket

For the dressing
2 tbsp runny honey
1 tsp ground cinnamon
1 tsp mustard powder
½ tsp sea salt
½ tsp freshly ground black pepper
4 tbsp cider vinegar
4 tbsp sunflower or other neutral-flavoured oil

★ ★ ★ ★ ★ ★ ★ ★ ★ ★ ★ ★ ★ ★ ★ ★ ★ ★ ★

First, make the dressing. Whisk the honey, cinnamon, mustard, salt and pepper together to create a thick paste. Gradually whisk in the vinegar, followed by the oil. (If making in advance, store the dressing in a sealed jar and refrigerate. It will keep for 1–2 weeks).

Assemble the salad when you are nearly ready to serve. Toss the pineapple, prawns, palm hearts, mint and parsley together in large bowl. Add the rocket and half the dressing and gently toss again. Divide the salad among individual bowls and drizzle over a little more dressing. Serve immediately.

Brasilian desserts are a combination of traditional Portuguese puddings brought over during the colonization, and indigenous Brasilian ingredients such as coconut, nuts and banana. Traditional dishes often have quirky and wonderfully descriptive names, such as Anthill Cake, which is flecked with chocolate, and Hoping For a Husband Cake.

Puddings are usually very sweet – many are made with condensed milk – and you'll also find a variety of smaller candies that are great for children to make. The hot climate means that ice creams are available in abundance in a wide variety of flavours, including native Amazonian fruits (see page 162).

DESSERTS, SWEETS & TREATS

CRAZY LADY CAKE

SERVES 8-10

This dense, dark, flourless chocolate cake, called *nega maluca* in Brasil, is, according to some people, often served at parties to absorb all the alcohol! Try it with a scoop of vanilla or coconut ice cream to offset the chocolate.

360g good-quality dark chocolate
200g golden caster sugar
200g butter
3 large eggs, separated
150g ground almonds
pinch of sea salt

★ ★ ★ ★ ★ ★ ★ ★ ★ ★ ★ ★ ★ ★ ★ ★ ★ ★ ★

Preheat the oven to 170°C/325°F/Gas mark 3. Grease and line a deep, round 20cm diameter springform cake tin. Break the chocolate into small pieces and place in a heatproof bowl along with the sugar and butter. Place over a pan of barely simmering water, making sure that the bottom of the bowl does not touch the water. Stir until the chocolate and butter have melted and the mixture is smooth.

Remove the bowl from the pan and leave to cool slightly. Fold in the egg yolks, followed by the ground almonds. Put the egg whites and salt into a large bowl and whisk to soft peaks. Fold this through the chocolate mixture. Spread the mixture evenly into the prepared tin, then place it on a large baking tray. Bake for 45–55 minutes, until the cake is just set but still quite moist in the middle. It should be firm on top but have a very slight wobble underneath when you gently shake it, and a few crumbs should stick to a skewer inserted into the middle of the cake.

Remove from the oven and immediately drape a clean kitchen towel over it (this will help prevent the top from becoming too crusty). Leave to cool completely before unmoulding to serve.

BRIGADEIROS

Brigadeiros were created by the wife of Brigadier Eduardo Gomes, who was a presidential candidate in the 1940s. She would serve the truffles at his fundraising events, and guests loved them so much that people soon started asking: 'Have you tried the Brigadeiro's sweets?' The name eventually stuck. They're easy to prepare, and perfect for making with kids.

400g condensed milk
4 tbsp cocoa powder
¼ tsp sea salt
3 tbsp butter
1 vanilla pod
good-quality chocolate sprinkles,
    for coating

★ ★ ★ ★ ★ ★ ★ ★ ★ ★ ★ ★ ★ ★ ★ ★ ★ ★ ★ ★

Pour the condensed milk into a heavy-based saucepan and sift in the cocoa powder and salt. Place over a low heat and cook for 10–15 minutes, stirring, until the mixture is thick, shiny and leaves the sides of the pan when stirred. Do not leave the pan unattended, as the condensed milk can burn easily.

Once the chocolate mixture has thickened, remove from the heat and stir in the butter. Split the vanilla pod in half lengthways and scrape out the seeds with the back of a small knife. Add the seeds to the pan and stir well. (The scraped-out pod can be used to make vanilla sugar – just put it in your sugar jar and leave it to infuse the sugar). Let the mixture cool completely, then cover with clingfilm and chill for about 30 minutes, until set.

Put the chocolate sprinkles in a small bowl. If you have one, use a mini ice-cream scoop to make a 20g ball and drop it into the sprinkles (alternatively, use a teaspoon). Coat it liberally with the sprinkles, roll it with your hands to make a neat ball and place it in a mini cupcake or petit-four case. Continue with the rest of the mixture. Store in an airtight container in the fridge, but take them out at least half an hour before serving, as they're best at room temperature.

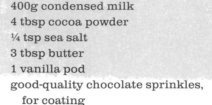

134

BEIJINHOS

MAKES ABOUT 25

Beijinhos, or 'little kisses', are pretty coconut candies traditionally studded with a single clove. They're a perfect handmade treat for handing out at parties or as a gift. If you're feeling adventurous, you could use the finely grated flesh of a fresh coconut.

400g condensed milk
2 tbsp butter, plus extra for greasing
pinch of sea salt
200g desiccated coconut
handful of cloves, to decorate (optional)

Put the condensed milk, butter, salt and 150g coconut in a heavy-based saucepan and stir well. Cook, stirring frequently, over a medium heat for 10–15 minutes, until the mixture thickens and comes away from the sides of the pan. Do not leave the pan unattended, as the condensed milk can burn easily. When ready, remove the pan from the heat.

Lightly butter a shallow dish, pour in the mixture and leave to cool completely. Cover with clingfilm and chill for at least 15 minutes to let the mixture firm up a little.

To shape the *beijinhos*, spread the remaining coconut in a shallow bowl. With damp or lightly oiled hands, roll the mixture into 20g balls about 2.5cm in diameter, then roll in the coconut. Place each ball in a mini cupcake or petit-four case and stud with a single clove to decorate, if you like. They are best served slightly chilled, but are also good at room temperature.

PÉ DE MOLEQUE

SERVES 4–6

During the colonial era, Brasilian streets were paved with stones placed over a thin layer of sand, which the street children would stamp down, and this nut brittle has a similar appearance to those stone pavements, hence the name *pé de moleque*, which means 'urchin's foot'. It's traditionally made with peanuts, but we've used cashew nuts as a homage to another of Brasil's favourite nuts. *Rapadura* (see page 9) is a basic form of sugar made from sugar cane juice.

300g rapadura (or soft, light muscovado sugar)
150g roasted cashew nuts
pinch of sea salt

★ ★ ★ ★ ★ ★ ★ ★ ★ ★ ★ ★ ★ ★ ★ ★ ★ ★ ★ ★

Line a baking sheet with a silicone liner or lightly grease it with butter.

If using rapadura, chop it into small pieces. Place the sugar in a large heavy-based saucepan and pour in 125ml water. Stir once or twice over a low heat to dissolve the sugar, then increase the heat slightly and simmer for 15–25 minutes, until it reaches the hard ball stage (120–130°C/250–265°F on a sugar thermometer). Monitor it carefully, as the syrup can easily boil over if the heat is too high. If you don't have a sugar thermometer, check by dropping a little of the syrup into a glass of cold water. It should cool into a hard but malleable ball that will change shape when you squeeze it with your fingers.

Remove from the heat and add the cashew nuts and salt. Stir until the nuts are evenly coated. Pour the mixture on to the prepared baking sheet and smooth it out with a spatula or lightly oiled palette knife. Leave to cool and harden completely.

To serve, break the hardened brittle into shards with the tip of a knife. If not serving immediately, store in an airtight container between sheets of greaseproof paper. It's great with strong black coffee.

'URCHIN'S FOOT' PAVING STONES IN PARATY, BRASIL

DESSERTS, SWEETS & TREATS

BANANA UPSIDE-DOWN CAKE

SERVES 8–10

In Brasil there are many types of banana cakes: *cuca*, a German cake with a rich, crumbly topping; banana bread; *bolo* cakes, which are sometimes made in a ring shape and often spread with cinnamon; and our favourite, the upside-down cake. Like the French tarte tatin, this indulgent cake is cooked with a layer of caramelized bananas at the bottom, then turned upside-down to show its sticky-sweet banana topping. Perfect as a teatime treat.

For the banana caramel
300g caster sugar
4–5 ripe bananas
¼ tsp cinnamon

For the cake batter
140g soft unsalted butter, plus extra for greasing
180g plain flour
1½ tsp baking powder
1 tsp ground cinnamon
4 eggs, separated
140g golden caster sugar
2 large ripe bananas, peeled and mashed

Preheat the oven to 170°C/325°F/Gas mark 3. Generously butter the base and sides of a heavy-based 23cm diameter springform cake tin, then line it with baking parchment.

To make the banana caramel, put the sugar and 150ml water in a heavy-based saucepan and cook over a high heat until the sugar has dissolved. Let it boil until thickened to a golden-brown caramel, taking care not to burn it. Remove and immediately pour it into the cake tin, tipping the tin slightly from side to side until evenly coated. Peel the bananas and halve them lengthways. Arrange them over the caramel in a neat pattern, trimming as necessary, then dust with the ground cinnamon.

Sift together the flour, baking powder and cinnamon into a bowl. Put the egg whites in a separate clean bowl and whisk to stiff peaks. Put the butter and sugar in another large bowl and whisk until light and fluffy. Slowly whisk in the egg yolks one at a time. Fold in the mashed bananas, followed by the dry ingredients. Finally, fold in the egg whites.

Pour the batter into the tin and spread evenly with a spatula. Bake for 50–60 minutes, or until a skewer inserted into the centre comes out clean. Remove and leave to cool for a few minutes before unmoulding. (It is easier to unmould while it is still warm, before the caramel base hardens). Run a thin knife around the inside of the tin. Put a large flat plate over the top and, holding the tin and the plate, invert it, gently lift off the tin and peel off the baking parchment. Serve warm.

HOW TO SAMBA

Samba is the beat of Brasil and the heart of Carnaval, Brasil's biggest and most famous festival. The dance has African origins, and is characterized by sensual hip movements and the flirtatious passion of the dance partners. The dance is so integral to Brasil that most cities have their own *sambadromo*, a specially built exhibition space for the local samba schools to perform and compete in.

Here are the basic samba moves for you to try. The rhythm is '1-and-2, 3-and-4'. Practise it slowly to begin with, then you can gradually build up speed.

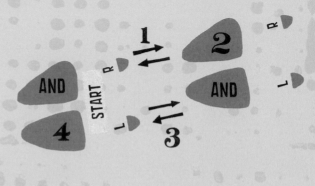

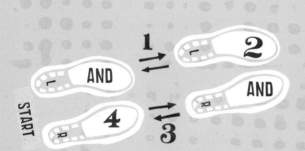

MAN

WOMAN

Step forward with your left foot (count 1)	Step backward with your right foot (count 1)
Move your right foot to your left foot (and)	Move your left foot to your right foot (and)
Left foot in place, weight shifts to it (count 2)	Right foot in place, weight shifts to it (count 2)
Step backward with your right foot (count 3)	Step forward with your left foot (count 3)
Move your left foot to your right foot (and)	Move your right foot to your left foot (and)
Right foot in place, weight shifts to it (count 4)	Left foot in place, weight shifts to it (count 4)

142

Now you have the moves, try out your footwork
with the top ten tracks on the Cabana jukebox:

MAS QUE NADA
Sérgio Mendes feat. The Black Eyed Peas
★ ★ ★ ★

SUN IS SHINING
Bebel Gilberto
★ ★ ★ ★

NOVA BOSSA NOVA
Marcos Valle
★ ★ ★ ★

GHOST TOWN
Veep
★ ★ ★ ★

MENINHA
Nu Braz
★ ★ ★ ★

CALIFORNIAN SOUL
Wilson das Neves
★ ★ ★ ★

EMORIO
Sérgio Mendes
★ ★ ★ ★

SUMMERTIME
Rosinha de Valença
★ ★ ★ ★

BRASILIAN LOVE SONG
Nat King Cole
★ ★ ★ ★

TAKE ME BACK TO PIAUI
Juca Chaves

BRASIL NUT BANOFFEE PIE

SERVES 10

Brasil nuts are called *castanhas do Pará* in Brasil, which means 'chestnuts from Pará', the northern state where they are most readily grown. Here we've used them in the base of our Banoffee Pie, an incredibly simple but delicious banana and toffee pie with a thick whipped cream topping. It's best on the day you make it, but any leftovers can be kept chilled for up to three days.

200g digestive biscuits
50g Brasil nuts, roughly chopped
60g unsalted butter, melted
1 egg
400g Doce de Leite (opposite), or use ready-made condensed milk caramel
300ml double cream
1 tsp vanilla extract
3 firm ripe bananas
½ lime
50g good-quality dark chocolate

★ ★ ★ ★ ★ ★ ★ ★ ★ ★ ★ ★ ★ ★ ★ ★

Preheat the oven to 180°C/350°F/Gas mark 4. Break the biscuits into small pieces and place in a food processor. Add the nuts and process until it resembles fine breadcrumbs. Add the melted butter and egg and blend until the mixture just starts to come together. Scrape the mixture into a 24cm diameter tart tin with a removable base. Press it evenly over the base and sides with the back of a spoon or a spatula. Put the tin on a baking sheet and bake for 15–20 minutes, until lightly golden. Remove and leave to cool completely, then chill for at least 1 hour until firm.

Spread two thirds of the Doce de Leite evenly over the pie crust base. Whip the double cream and vanilla extract to soft peaks. Peel and slice the bananas into rounds, then squeeze over a little lime juice to prevent them from browning. Neatly arrange the banana slices over the caramel. Spread the whipped cream over the banana layer. Grate the chocolate into a small bowl and sprinkle it over the cream to decorate, then drizzle with the remaining Doce de Leite. Carefully unmould the pie from the tin and transfer to a cake plate to serve.

DOCE DE LEITE

MAKES 400G

Doce de leite, better known by its Spanish name, *dulce de leche*, is a sticky sweet caramel sauce. It can be made from scratch, or by using this Brasilian cooks' short-cut: slowly boiling a can of condensed milk. You can use it as a breakfast spread, a dip for fruit, or for any recipes requiring caramel or melted toffee.

1 x 400g tin condensed milk

Remove the label from the tin and place it in a small, deep pan. Pour in enough water to cover the tin, then bring to the boil. Reduce the heat to a simmer and cover with a lid. Cook for just under 3 hours, occasionally topping up the water and checking that the top of the can is still submerged. Do take care here; if the lid is exposed, it may explode!

After 3 hours, carefully remove the tin from the pan and pat dry. Leave to cool before opening to use.

The longer you cook the condensed milk for, the firmer or lumpier it becomes. After 3 hours you'll have a thick, caramel-like sauce, (there may be lumps at the bottom, but you can stir it to smooth them out). If you cook it for ½–1 hour longer you can eat it with a spoon as a pudding, use it to sandwich biscuits together for a Brasilian-style custard cream, or even to make fudge. If the consistency is a bit too thick, just stir in some boiling water.

ROMEU E JULIETA PASTEL

MAKES 12–14

Romeu e Julieta (Romeo and Juliet) is the Brasilian name for the contrasting combination of sweet red *goiabada* (guava paste) and salty white cheese. You can find it in all manner of desserts, from mousses and ice cream to cheesecake and tarts, but our favourite is as a filling for *pastels*. The bubbly pastry allows the filling to melt softly – just make sure they're not too hot!

250g plain flour
¼ tsp bicarbonate of soda
½ tsp fine sea salt
½ tsp caster sugar
40g lard, melted
1½ tsp cider vinegar
1 shot cachaça (about 35ml) or vodka
100g guava paste (*goiabada*) or quince paste (*membrillo*), cut in small pieces
50g cream cheese
50g ricotta
vegetable oil, for deep-frying
icing sugar and cinnamon, for dusting (optional)

★ ★ ★ ★ ★ ★ ★ ★ ★ ★ ★ ★ ★ ★ ★ ★ ★ ★ ★

To make the dough, put the flour, bicarbonate of soda, salt and sugar in a large bowl. In a small bowl, mix the lard, vinegar, cachaça and about 40ml lukewarm water together. Add this to the flour and mix together to form a soft dough. If the dough is too dry and won't form a ball, keep adding more water a little at a time until it comes together. Tip on to a lightly floured surface and knead briefly until smooth. (Try not to overwork it or it will become tough). Cover with clingfilm and let it rest for 1 hour.

On a lightly floured surface, roll out half the dough into a thin rectangle, then cut out rough 9–10cm squares. Mix the guava paste with the cream cheese and ricotta in a small bowl. Put a teaspoon of the filling in the middle of a pastry square. Brush around the filling with a little water, then fold it over into a rectangle and seal it. Use a 7–8cm round pastry cutter to cut the pastel into a semi-circle or half moon shape and seal the edge with the tines of a fork. Transfer to a tray lined with greaseproof paper. Continue making pastels until all the filling has been used up.

Heat the oil in a deep-fat fryer to about 180°C/350°F (a little dough dropped into the hot oil should immediately sizzle). Fry in batches for 2–3 minutes, without overcrowding the pan, until golden on both sides. Remove and drain on kitchen paper. Keep warm while you fry the rest. Serve warm as they are, or dusted with icing sugar and cinnamon, if you like.

146

PASSION FRUIT PUDIM

SERVES 8

Pudim is one of Brasil's most famous desserts. It originated in Portugal and its name derives from the English word 'pudding'. Known in other countries as flan or crème caramel, it's a baked custard, often made with condensed milk in Brasil, topped with caramel sauce. There are many variations of *pudim* – some are made with coconut, fruits or nuts, but our favourite is this version speckled with passion fruit seeds.

oil or butter, for greasing
320g caster sugar
8 ripe passion fruit
150ml double cream
300ml whole milk
150ml coconut milk
1 vanilla pod
4 eggs

★ ★ ★ ★ ★ ★ ★ ★ ★ ★ ★ ★ ★ ★ ★ ★ ★ ★ ★ ★

Preheat the oven to 150°C/300°F/Gas mark 2, lightly oil or butter 8 individual dariole moulds or ramekins, then put them in a deep roasting tray.

To make the caramel, put 200g of the sugar and 100ml water in a heavy-based saucepan and cook over a low heat until the sugar has dissolved. Increase the heat and boil for 5–10 minutes, without stirring, until golden brown. Remove from the heat and carefully pour the caramel into the prepared ramekins. It will harden as it cools. Halve 4 of the passion fruit and scoop out the juice and pulp into the moulds, over the caramel.

Next, make the custard. Pour the double cream, milk and coconut milk into a saucepan. Split the vanilla pod lengthways and scrape out the seeds with the back of the knife. Add both to the saucepan and slowly bring to a simmer. When it begins to rise up the sides of the pan, remove from the heat.

Split the remaining passion fruit, scoop out the pulp and strain the juice into a bowl. Whisk the remaining sugar, eggs and passion fruit juice in a large bowl. Gradually trickle in the hot milk and cream, stirring constantly. Pour the mixture through a fine sieve into a large jug.

Divide the custard between the moulds and carefully place the tray on the bottom oven shelf. Pull out the shelf slightly and pour hot water into the tray until it reaches halfway up the sides of the moulds. Bake for 40–45 minutes, until just set. They should have a slight wobble when you gently shake the tray. Remove and carefully transfer the ramekins to a cooling rack. Once cooled, chill in the fridge for at least 4 hours. To unmould, run a knife around the insides of the ramekins. Dip in a bowl of very hot water for about 10 seconds and invert on to a small plate. Serve immediately.

AVOCADO ICE CREAM

MAKES ABOUT 1.2 LITRES (SERVES 10–12)

Avocado is eaten as a fruit in Brasil, so don't be surprised if you see it popping up on dessert menus. It's popular in mousses, but we like it best in ice cream, as its richness results in a wonderfully smooth texture. It might sound odd at first, but do give this a go – it's truly delicious.

250g caster sugar
zest and juice of 2 lemons
zest and juice of 2 limes
200ml double cream
600ml whole milk
4 large ripe avocados
pinch of fine sea salt

Put the sugar and lemon and lime zest and juice in a heavy-based saucepan. Slowly bring to the boil, stirring to dissolve the sugar. Once the sugar has melted, add the cream and stir well. Gradually bring to the boil. As soon as it starts to bubble up, remove the pan from the heat and pour in the milk. Halve the avocados, then remove the stones, scoop out the flesh and place in a food processor or blender. Pour in the milk and cream mixture and blitz until smooth, scraping the sides to make sure there are no chunks of avocado left.

Pour the mixture into the bowl of an ice-cream machine and churn until almost set (or according to the manufacturer's instructions). Transfer to a clean plastic container and freeze for at least a few hours until firm. (If you do not have an ice-cream maker, freeze the mixture in a shallow plastic container. Take it out after a couple of hours and whisk it by hand or with an electric whisk. Repeat the process twice, then return the ice cream to the freezer for a final freeze.)

COCONUT & LIME SORBET

MAKES ABOUT 1 LITRE (SERVES 6–8)

This refreshing sorbet is perfect for a hot day. The lime's tartness cuts through the coconut cream to create a tangy treat that will give you dreams of suntan lotion and palm trees.

300g caster sugar
juice of 3 and finely grated zest of 4 limes
750ml coconut cream

Put a large freezerproof bowl in the freezer. Put the sugar, lime juice and 250ml coconut cream in a saucepan, place over a high heat and stir to encourage the sugar to dissolve. Bring to a simmer and cook for about 5 minutes, until thickened slightly. Remove from the heat and stir in the remaining coconut cream. Pour the mixture through a fine sieve into the chilled bowl, pressing through any lumps of coconut cream, then add the lime zest.

Pour the mixture into an ice-cream maker and churn until you get a soft sorbet consistency. Transfer to a clean plastic container and freeze for a few hours until the sorbet is firm. (If you do not have an ice-cream maker, freeze the mixture in a shallow plastic container. Take it out after a couple of hours and whisk it by hand or with an electric whisk. Repeat the process twice, then return the sorbet to the freezer for a final freeze).

To make it easier to scoop, put the sorbet in the fridge for 30 minutes to allow it to soften slightly before serving.

CAIPIRINHA GRANITA

MAKES ABOUT 600ML (SERVES 6)

As you may have noticed, we're rather partial to a caipirinha, whether it's in a glass, on a roast chicken (page 58), or in a granita. Alcohol can be tricky because it freezes at a lower temperature than water, so this is the best way to enjoy a frozen caipirinha. And the best part is that it's dead simple to do.

100g caster sugar
100ml fresh lime juice (2½ large limes)
200ml cachaça
freshly grated lime zest, to serve
cachaça, to serve

Put 200ml water and the sugar in a saucepan and stir over a high heat until the sugar has dissolved. Stop stirring and leave the syrup to simmer for a few minutes to thicken slightly. Remove the pan from the heat and add the lime juice and cachaça. Pour the mixture into a metal tray or a wide plastic container (with lid) and leave to cool completely.

Cover the tray with clingfilm and freeze for a few hours, until the mixture is frozen around the edges and slushy in the middle. Use a fork to break up the ice into smaller crystals. Return the tray to the freezer. Repeat this process 3 more times every ½–1 hour until the mixture is completely frozen and has the texture of snow.

When ready to serve, roughly fork up the granita, then spoon into chilled serving glasses. Sprinkle with a little lime zest and add a shot of cachaça, if you like.

SANTA MARTA

Haas & Hahn are Dutch artists Jeroen Koolhaas and
Dre Urhahn, who have made a name for themselves
by making art in some of the world's most dangerous
places. A documentary they filmed in Rio and São
Paulo in 2005 inspired them to start the Favela Painting
Project, where their aim has been to beautify and bring
positivity to Brasil's most deprived *favelas* (slums)
by engaging the local communities in painting the
buildings with startlingly bright and colourful murals.

For one of the projects, Haas & Hahn drew up a design to cover the main strip of 34 houses in the favela with 7,000 square metres of beautiful rainbow stripes. As part of the project Tudo de Cor para Santa Marta (Everything Colourful for Santa Marta), local inhabitants were instructed on everything from different types of paint to scaffolding, and their hard work was rewarded with a monthly paycheck. By the end of the project, the residents had gained new skills, some money and a dazzling new centre for the community. Santa Marta is now recognized as a model pacified *favela*, and we're delighted to showcase this amazing project – it's the inspiration for our bathrooms, where corrugated iron is covered with rays of pastel paint, and for the whole façade of one of our Cabanas.

With more than 120 different fruits native to its rainforests, it's no wonder that Brasil is teeming with fresh fruit juice bars. You find them on every street corner in Rio, their doors flung wide open on to the streets as Cariocas (natives of Rio) line the long counters, asking for myriad combinations of fruits in their *sucos* (juices) or *vitaminas* (thickened fruit shakes). Of course, once the sun goes down on Ipanema, these fruits play an even more important role in cocktails laced with cachaça, muddled with plenty of lime and sprinkled with cane sugar. Try these recipes from behind the bar at Cabana, or have a go at creating your own with any fruit you like.

JUICES, COCKTAILS & REFRESCOS

DRINKS TIPS & TRICKS

VANILLA SUGAR

You can buy vanilla sugar in supermarkets, but it's really easy to make it yourself: just put a couple of lightly bruised or scraped-out vanilla pods in a jar of sugar and leave to infuse for a few days.

CRACKED ICE

The weather is so hot in Brasil that crushed ice melts too quickly, so it's traditional to use cracked ice instead. For a truly authentic cocktail, you can make cracked ice by placing a handful of ice cubes in a clean plastic bag and bashing them into chunks using a rolling pin. You could also use a pestle and mortar or an ice cracker (see page 166).

GOMME SYRUP & SIMPLE SYRUP

Gomme syrup is a sweetener that's often used in bars and restaurants to make alcoholic cocktails, as it gives drinks a silky texture. At home, it can easily be substituted with a simple sugar syrup made from equal quantities of sugar and water heated over a medium heat until the sugar has dissolved.

STRAWBERRY PURÉE

To make your own strawberry purée, whizz a punnet of hulled and roughly chopped strawberries in a small blender. You can freeze it in an ice cube tray and use it when needed to make cocktails and smoothies.

BACANA BERRY REFRESCO

SERVES 1

Bacana means 'cool' in Portuguese, and this berry soda is not only refreshing, but is also easy to make, and looks beautiful in a clear glass garnished with fresh fruit. A *refresco* is a cold fruit drink that's sipped as an alternative to a *refrigerante* (a bottled or canned soft drink).

4 blackberries, plus extra to garnish (optional)
4 raspberries, plus extra to garnish (optional)
½ tsp vanilla sugar (page 159)
handful of cracked ice (page 159)
2 tbsp grapefruit juice
100ml lemonade
50ml soda water

★ ★ ★ ★ ★ ★ ★ ★ ★ ★ ★ ★ ★ ★ ★ ★

Muddle the berries with the vanilla sugar in a tall, sturdy glass, then fill with cracked ice until it is two-thirds full. Add the grapefruit juice and stir. Top with the lemonade and soda. Stir again and serve immediately, garnished with blackberries and raspberries if you like.

AMAZON ICED TEA

SERVES 2

With a climate that rarely dips below 20°C, it's no wonder that iced tea is a popular thirst-quencher in Brasil. There, it's often home-made with *mate*, a South American tea made from the leaves of the *erva-mate* plant. Green tea makes a great substitute.

100ml green tea, infused overnight
    and strained
200ml apple juice
50ml elderflower cordial
50ml lime juice
a few mint leaves
handful of ice cubes

★ ★ ★ ★ ★ ★ ★ ★ ★ ★ ★ ★ ★ ★ ★ ★

Put all the ingredients in a cocktail shaker and shake vigorously for a few minutes. Strain into chilled tall glasses or tumblers and top up with ice cubes. Serve immediately.

LIMONADA SUISSA

SERVES 1

At the turn of the nineteenth century, Swiss chocolatiers came to Brasil to make chocolate due to the abundance of cacao trees. They created this refreshing drink to cool them down in the hot climate.

½ lemon
½ lime
1 tbsp caster sugar, or to taste
handful of ice cubes
about 175ml soda water

★ ★ ★ ★ ★ ★ ★ ★ ★ ★ ★ ★ ★ ★ ★ ★

Cut the lemon and lime into small wedges and place them in a sturdy glass or tumbler. Add the sugar and muddle the ingredients until the sugar has dissolved. Fill the glass two-thirds full with ice, then top with soda water. Stir well and serve immediately.

LIMONADA
SUISSA

BACANA
BERRY
REFRESCO

AMAZON
ICED TEA

KEY TO PICTURE OPPOSITE

FIVE BRASILIAN FRUITS
YOU'VE PROBABLY NEVER HEARD OF

Since nearly all of its climate is tropical, Brasil boasts an enormous range of fruit. Some are probably familiar – there are pineapples, bananas and coconuts in abundance – and some you may even struggle to pronounce, such as *bocaiúva, jabuticaba* and *cupuaçu*. You now know all about *açaí* (see page 20), but here are some more of our favourite weird and wonderful Brasilian fruits.

ACEROLA

The *acerola* is a small, bright red berry that resembles a cherry. It's packed with so much vitamin C (over 30 times more than orange juice) that it's set to rival *açaí* as Brasil's best superfruit. The fruit itself has a bitter-sweet taste and can be eaten raw, but we've also tried it as an ice cream or in a blend of juices.

CAJU

Have you ever seen a picture of a cashew fruit? We thought not. In which case, it might surprise you to learn that cashew nuts are actually just the tip of the *caju*, or cashew fruit, and are encased in a black, kidney-bean shaped shell. The inside of this shell contains a horrible, corrosive liquid, but attached to the nut is a pear-shaped, red-and-yellow fruit known as the 'cashew apple'. The flesh is soft with a sweet but slightly astringent taste, a bit like an unripe apricot. As well as being eaten fresh, it's used in stews or to make jams and chutneys, but we've tried it most successfully in a *caipirinha de caju* – a cashew-fruit variation of the classic Brasilian cocktail.

GOIABA

The Brasilian guava, the *goiaba* is a round, green, white or yellow fruit with bright pink pulp that tastes like a mixture of mango, strawberry and pear. Brasilians like to eat it as a sweet paste (which is similar to the better-known membrillo, or quince jelly), and it's often combined with a hard white cheese called *minas* to spread on toast for breakfast. This combination is often called Romeu e Julieta because, despite the salty/sweet and red/white contrasts of the fruit and cheese, they're a marriage made in heaven.

JACA

The *jaca*, better known as jackfruit, is the world's largest edible fruit, and sometimes grows up to three feet long. Originally from Southeast Asia and India, it's not actually native to Brasil, but grows all over the tropical parts of the country. In Brasil there are three different varieties of the fruit, ranging from a hard, firm-fleshed variety (*jaca-dura*) to our favourite, the *jaca-mole*, which has the softest, sweetest flesh.

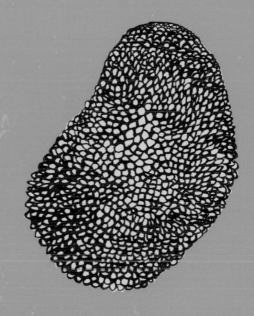

LICURI

We first tried *licuri* – a hard brown fruit that looks a bit like a hazelnut but is actually a tiny coconut – at innovative young Brasilian chef Felipe Bronze's Rio restaurant, Oro. The fruit can be eaten whole: it has a rough brown exterior that gives way to a fibrous, white, fleshy interior, which is sweet and has a subtle coconut flavour.

JUICES, COCKTAILS & REFRESCOS

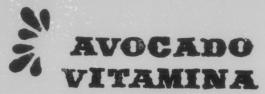

AVOCADO VITAMINA

SERVES 3–4

A *vitamina* is a type of fruit shake found in juice bars all over Brasil. Avocados are often used, and their rich flesh gives the drink a silky texture. They're full of nutrients such as fibre, potassium, vitamin E and folic acid – so this is not only delicious, but also good for you!

1 large avocado
1 large ripe banana
400ml whole or semi-skimmed milk
handful of ice cubes
3–4 tbsp runny honey, to taste
juice and grated zest of ½ lime

Halve and peel the avocado, remove the stone and chop the flesh into rough chunks. Peel and roughly chop the banana. Place them in a blender along with the rest of the ingredients and blend until smooth. Taste and adjust the sweetness with more honey or a squeeze of lime. Pour into chilled tall glasses or tumblers and sprinkle the lime zest on top. Serve immediately.

MANGO & COCONUT SMOOTHIE

SERVES 2

This thick smoothie is a real taste of the tropics: frozen mango and banana is blended with coconut milk and Greek yoghurt, sweetened with honey and sprinkled with cinnamon.

120g frozen mango chunks (or freeze fresh chopped mango overnight)
1 large banana, chopped and frozen overnight
165ml coconut milk
4 tbsp Greek yoghurt
2 tbsp runny honey
pinch ground cinnamon

Put all the ingredients except the cinnamon in a blender and process on high speed until the mixture is thick and smooth. If the mixture is too thick, add a splash of water or a few ice cubes and blend again. Pour into chilled glasses and serve immediately, with a sprinkling of cinnamon.

YOUR CAIPIRINHA KIT

Fancy becoming a caipirinha master? Here are the tools you'll need to perfect your skills.

 1 A SHOT MEASURER

Because you can have too much of a good thing.

 2 A SMALL SERRATED KNIFE

To slice your limes thinly.

 3 A SMALL WOODEN CHOPPING BOARD

For only the finest lime chopping.

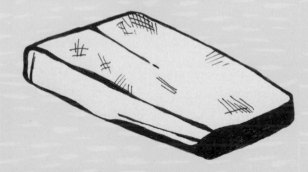

 4 AN ICE CRACKER

Ice for a caipirinha should be in rough chunks rather than crushed. Use an ice cracker or a rolling pin as described on page 159. If you can't find one, use a long metal spoon to crack your ice cubes into pieces.

 5 A DURABLE BASE FOR MUDDLING

So you won't ruin your caipirinha by breaking the glass through over-vigorous muddling.

 6 A WOODEN MUDDLER

To muddle your limes and sugar perfectly.

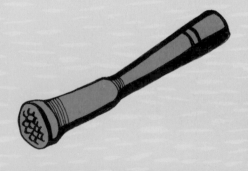

THE PERFECT CAIPIRINHA

SERVES 1

The *caipirinha*, which means 'little country girl' in Portuguese, is Brasil's national cocktail. There are many stories about how it was invented, but this is our favourite: in the olden days, people would press a cloth moistened with alcohol to their heads to reduce a fever and suck a lime to improve their immunity. One day, a feverish man found the alcohol on his forehead dripping into his mouth as he sucked a lime, and since it was bitter he ate a spoonful of sugar. He got better, and the caipirinha was born. You can use ordinary white or granulated sugar, but we like the slightly caramelized flavour of golden caster sugar. There are as many variations of fruit caipirinhas as there are fruit, but below are three of our favourites. Try experimenting to see what creations you can concoct.

1½ limes, skin on, cut into rough cubes
1 tbsp golden caster sugar
65ml cachaça (we like Velho Barreiro)
handful of cracked ice (see page 159)

★ ★ ★ ★ ★ ★ ★ ★ ★ ★ ★ ★ ★ ★ ★ ★ ★ ★ ★

Put the limes and sugar in a sturdy glass tumbler. Muddle them with a cocktail muddler or the end of a small rolling pin to extract the juice from the lime and dissolve the sugar. Add the cachaça and cracked ice and give it a stir. Finally, top the glass with more cracked ice and add a wooden lollipop stick for stirring. Serve immediately.

VARIATIONS

Strawberry & Lime Caipirinha

Add 3–4 strawberries to the limes before muddling, then proceed as above.

Pineapple & Mint Caipirinha

Replace the limes with 2 shredded mint leaves and 5 cubes of ripe pineapple, then proceed as above. Garnish with extra mint.

Passion Fruit Caipirinha

Replace the limes with the pulp of a passion fruit. Proceed as above and garnish with half a passion fruit.

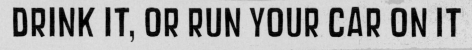

CACHAÇA:

DRINK IT, OR RUN YOUR CAR ON IT

Say it with us now: cachaça. *Ka-sha-sa*. It's the national drink of Brasil and the base of its best-known cocktail. Like rum, it's a sugar cane spirit, but unlike rum it's distilled directly from fermented sugar cane juice, rather than from the molasses (the syrupy by-product that's created when sugar cane is turned into sugar).

Also like rum, cachaça comes in a variety of styles and characters, from the un-aged spirit to the more sophisticated, matured, artisanal product. The common 'white' cachaça was originally considered only a poor man's drink, no better than hooch. It is often given the slang name *pinga* (from the Portuguese *pingar*, to drip, referring to the distillation process), and is a clear, strong spirit with a grassy flavour that's perfect for mixing and cocktails. However, there has recently been a surge in the production of mature cachaça, which is aged in wooden barrels, is darker in colour and has more mellow flavours, such as cinnamon, vanilla and dried fruits. This can be sipped on its own and makes a great alternative to an after-dinner brandy or whisky.

A short time ago it would have been hard to get your hands on a bottle of cachaça unless you'd conveniently been on a trip to Brasil or Portugal. However, now that the spirit is gaining popularity, it should be simple to find brands such as Sagatiba, especially in larger supermarkets. If you're at a loss or simply don't like the taste of cachaça (some people can find it too rough or strong), you can always substitute vodka or rum – we won't tell!

Oh, and Brasilians really do sometimes run their cars on it. If you're ever crossing the road in Brasil and notice a waft of sweetness in the air, that's the ethanol from sugar cane. That probably isn't one to try at home...

159

BLOODY MARIA

SERVES 1

Our take on a Bloody Mary uses cachaça as the alcohol base, and features Cabana's own Bloody Maria mix, which includes Tabasco, mustard and horseradish for extra kick.

½ lime
1 tsp caster sugar, or to taste
handful of crushed ice
35ml cachaça
25ml Bloody Maria mix (opposite)
50ml tomato juice

Cut the lime into 4 wedges, leaving the skins on. Place in a tall, sturdy glass with the sugar. Muddle them with a cocktail muddler or the end of a small rolling pin to extract the juice from the lime and dissolve the sugar. Fill the glass half full with crushed ice, then stir in the cachaça and Bloody Maria mix. Fill to the top with tomato juice and a little more crushed ice, if you like. Stir well and serve immediately.

BLOODY MARIA MIX

MAKES ABOUT 175ML (7 SERVINGS)

145ml Worcestershire sauce
1 tsp creamed horseradish
2 tsp Tabasco
½ tsp finely ground mixed peppercorns
1 tsp celery salt
½ tsp sea salt
1 garlic clove, finely crushed
1 tsp English mustard
1 tsp balsamic vinegar

Mix all the ingredients together in a small jar with lid and keep chilled until ready to use. The mixture keeps well in the fridge for a few days.

STRAWBERRY BATIDA

WATERMELON MARTINI

BLOODY MARIA

KEY TO PICTURE OPPOSITE

STRAWBERRY BATIDA

SERVES 2

The *batida* is another classic Brasilian cocktail. It literally means 'shaken', and it's a bit like an alcoholic milkshake: lighter than a caipirinha and thickened with coconut milk. You can make it in advance and keep it in the fridge until ready to serve.

130ml cachaça
100g hulled strawberries, plus extra to garnish
50ml coconut cream
juice of 1 lime
4 tsp caster sugar
handful of ice cubes

★ ★ ★ ★ ★ ★ ★ ★ ★ ★ ★ ★ ★ ★ ★ ★ ★ ★

Place 2 glasses in the freezer to chill. Put all the ingredients (except the strawberries to garnish) in a blender with a handful of ice cubes. Blend at medium speed until smooth, then pour into the chilled glasses. Garnish each glass with a fresh strawberry and serve immediately.

WATERMELON MARTINI

SERVES 1

Lizzy drank this at Bar Astor in Ipanema on her first night in Rio, and instantly knew she was in Brasil. When we got home we were determined to recreate it, and here's the result: the flavour of hot summer nights.

5 small chunks fresh, ripe watermelon (skin removed), plus extra to garnish
35ml vodka
15ml cloudy apple juice
10ml passion fruit liqueur (or substitute vodka)
10ml watermelon syrup or simple sugar syrup (page 159), plus extra for drizzling
handful of ice cubes

★ ★ ★ ★ ★ ★ ★ ★ ★ ★ ★ ★ ★ ★ ★ ★ ★ ★

Place a martini glass in the freezer for 20 minutes to get it well chilled and frosty. Muddle the watermelon in the bottom of a cocktail shaker with a cocktail muddler or the end of a small rolling pin, leaving in any pips. Add the remaining ingredients with a handful of ice cubes, then cover the cocktail shaker and shake vigorously for a few seconds. Double-strain it into the chilled glass, making sure there are no pips.

Garnish with a slice of watermelon or 3 small watermelon balls on a cocktail stick. If you have watermelon syrup to hand, drizzle a little over the watermelon garnish, then serve immediately.

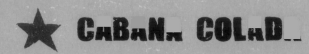

CaBaNa COLaDa

SERVES 2

This is our version of a piña colada, and uses cachaça and lots of lime for a citrus kick. For a virgin Cabana Colada, which is also very good, just leave out the cachaça.

2 tbsp coconut cream
2 tbsp lemon juice
2 tbsp simple sugar syrup (page 159)
4 tbsp pineapple juice
110ml coconut water
35ml cachaça
large handful of ice cubes
sprigs of mint, to garnish

Place 2 tall glasses in the freezer to chill. Put all the ingredients except the mint in a blender with a large handful of ice cubes. Blend well to a smooth, silky consistency. Pour into the chilled glasses, garnish with the mint sprigs and serve.

LYCHEE SAKENINHA

SERVES 1

This is one of the most popular cocktails in the clubs of São Paulo, which has the largest Japanese community in the country, and therefore a ready supply of sake. It's made the same way as a caipirinha, but uses sake instead of cachaça, and lychees for a sweet, perfumed flavour.

5 tinned lychees, drained, plus extra
   to garnish
2–4 tbsp lychee syrup from the tin, to taste
120ml sake
handful of cracked ice (page 159)

★ ★ ★ ★ ★ ★ ★ ★ ★ ★ ★ ★ ★ ★ ★

Muddle the lychees and lychee syrup with a cocktail muddler or the end of a small rolling pin in a tall, sturdy glass. Add sake and cracked ice. Give it a quick stir, then garnish with a lychee. Serve immediately.

BRASILIAN STREET FOOD PARTY

Take your friends on a trip to a São Paulo street market with this fun twist on a drinks and canapé party. There are plenty of things you can make ahead so that you're not stuck in the kitchen when all the fun is happening outside. To serve 8–10, you'll need to double the quantities of the Salmon Ceviche, Sweetcorn Soup Shots, Chicken 'Espírito Santo'. The quantities of caipirinhas we'll leave to you!

MENU

SALMON CEVICHE
(PAGE 42)

SWEETCORN SOUP SHOTS
(PAGE 38)

PÃO DE QUEIJO
(PAGE 27)

COXINHAS
(PAGE 26)

BOLINHOS
(PAGE 31)
WITH CHILLI MAYONNAISE
(PAGE 86)

CHICKEN 'ESPÍRITO SANTO'
WITH TOMATO & PEANUT SAUCE
(PAGE 48)

BEIJINHOS
(PAGE 135)

BRIGADEIROS
(PAGE 134)

DIY CAIPIRINHAS
(PAGE 168)

WITH THE INVITATIONS

+ Ask guests to bring along their favourite fruit to experiment with DIY caipirinhas in an assortment of fruit flavours.

THE DAY BEFORE

+ Make the Sweetcorn Soup and set aside in the fridge.

✕ Make the Beijinhos and Brigadeiros and store in airtight containers in the fridge.

✕ Prepare the Coxinhas and Bolinhos, then refrigerate, ready to deep-fry the next day.

✕ Make the Tomato & Peanut Sauce and Chilli Mayonnaise and set aside in the fridge.

FOUR HOURS BEFORE GUESTS ARRIVE

+ Freeze the salmon for 30 minutes, then slice thinly, cover and refrigerate.

✕ Make the Pão de Queijo and chill, ready to bake.

+ Prepare the Chicken 'Espírito Santo' skewers, cover and refrigerate.

✕ Make the Molho Vinagrete for the Sweetcorn Soup Shots.

ONE HOUR BEFORE GUESTS ARRIVE

+ Deep-fry the Coxinhas and Bolinhos and keep warm, covered, in a low oven.

HALF AN HOUR BEFORE GUESTS ARRIVE

✕ Set up a caipirinha bar with all the ingredients for Classic Caipirinhas, a few varieties of fruits and a set of instructions for guests to make their own caipirinhas.

✕ Bake the Pão de Queijo and keep warm in the oven.

+ Dress the Salmon Ceviche, then arrange in tiny bowls or soup spoons.

WHEN GUESTS ARRIVE

+ Encourage guests to make their own caipirinhas, adding their favourite fruit to the selection.

✕ Reheat the Sweetcorn Soup and serve in espresso cups with garnishes.

+ Bake the Chicken 'Espirito Santo' skewers and reheat the Tomato & Peanut Sauce.

✕ Serve some canapés every five minutes or so.

✕ When ready for dessert, serve the Beijinhos and Brigadeiros with strong coffee.

179

QUENTÃO

SERVES 4–5

The *quentão* (which means 'big hot one'), is a warm mulled drink that's usually served at winter festivals such as the Festa Junina.

110g vanilla sugar
4 cinnamon sticks, broken in half
4 cloves
3–4 slices fresh root ginger
peel of 1 small lemon
peel of 1 small orange
75ml orange juice
210ml cachaça
12 raspberries

Put the vanilla sugar in a large pan and add the cinnamon sticks, cloves, ginger and 800ml hot water. Twist the lemon and orange peels to release their fragrant oils and add them to the pan. Place over a medium heat and heat gently until the sugar has completely dissolved – this should take about 5 minutes. Once the sugar has dissolved, reduce the heat and add the orange juice, cachaça and raspberries. Heat gently for another 5 minutes. It's important not to let it boil or all the alcohol will be burnt off.

Ladle it into individual heatproof glasses and serve hot. If you're worried about whether your glasses will withstand the heat, put a tablespoon in each glass before you pour in the hot liquid; this will help disperse the heat.

CABANA PIMM'S

SERVES 4

RIO 2014

SERVES 4

The guarana is an indigenous red berry that's known for its stimulating effect. It's the main ingredient in the fizzy 'natural' energy drink called Guarana, which is becoming better known outside Brasil. We use it to replace the usual lemonade in Pimm's for a twist on the quintessential English drink.

100ml Pimm's No.1
2 x 330ml cans Guarana Antarctica
   (or any brand of fizzy Guarana)
ice cubes
2 passion fruit
½ cucumber, sliced
2 kiwis, skinned and cubed
handful of mint leaves

★ ★ ★ ★ ★ ★ ★ ★ ★ ★ ★ ★ ★ ★ ★ ★ ★

Combine the Pimm's and Guarana in a large jug and top with generous handfuls of ice cubes. Scoop the flesh out of the passion fruits and add to the jug with the cucumber slices, passion fruit, kiwi and mint leaves to garnish, and serve immediately.

Rio 2014 is our tribute to the World Cup, and our take on Sangria: a red wine punch with an added slug of cachaça. It's great for sharing and for celebrating with, so enjoy it with friends over a long evening in the sun.

ice cubes
150ml cachaça
225ml orange juice
110ml lemon juice
100ml simple sugar syrup (page 159)
225ml red wine
1 orange, sliced
1 lemon, sliced
small handful of mint leaves

★ ★ ★ ★ ★ ★ ★ ★ ★ ★ ★ ★ ★ ★ ★ ★ ★

Fill a large jug with ice cubes, then add the cachaça, orange and lemon juice and sugar syrup. Give the mixture a stir, then pour in the red wine. If you like, pour the red wine over the back of a tablespoon to create distinct layers within the jug. Garnish with the orange and lemon slices and mint leaves and serve immediately.

HOW THE SCOTS BROUGHT
FUTEBOL TO BRASIL

Futebol is integral to Brasilian culture and the popular image we have of Brasilians. And no wonder: they're the only team to have qualified for the World Cup every single year, they've won the tournament five times, and produced football legends such as Pelé, Garrincha, Ronaldo and Ronaldinho.

But actually, if it wasn't for the Scots, the Brasilians would never have learned how to play their beloved game. In fact, they owe the introduction of the game itself to a young Scotsman who stepped off a boat in Santos in 1894 with two footballs and a copy of the rulebook.

Charles Miller was the son of a Scottish railway engineer and a Brasilian mother, and was sent off to boarding school in Hampshire aged nine. When he returned to Brasil, all he had really learned, he later claimed, was a love of the game of football. He went on to help organize the first league in São Paulo at the turn of the last century, and even contributed the name Corinthians to São Paulo's top team. There is a street named after him, the Praça Charles Miller, and even a trick, the *chaleira*, in which a ball is flicked up behind the leg.

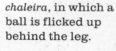

If you ever find yourself at a Brasilian football match, get into the spirit by learning these chants. (Note: Mengão is a nickname for the most famous Brasilian football team, Flamengo, who wear an iconic red and black shirt.)

DA-LHE, DA-LHE, DA-LHE, ÔÔÔ MENGÃO, DO MEU CORAÇÃO!

(Give it to them, give it to them, give it to them, ooooh Mengão, with all my heart!)

ÔÔ MEU MENGÃO, EU GOSTO DE VOCÊ / QUERO CANTAR AO MUNDO INTEIRO / A ALEGRIA DE SER RUBRO-NEGRO / CANTE COMIGO MENGÃO / ACIMA DE TUDO RUBRO-NEGRO

(Oh my Mengão, I love you. I want to sing it to the whole world. I'm so happy to be a red and black. Sing with me Mengão. Red and black above all else!)

MENGÃO, ESTOU SEMPRE CONTIGO / SOMOS UMA NAÇÃO / NÃO IMPORTA ONDE ESTEJA / SEMPRE ESTAREI CONTIGO

(Mengão, I'm always with you, we are one nation! It doesn't matter where we are, I am always with you.)

VAMOS FLAMENGO / VAMOS SER CAMPEÕES VAMOS FLAMENGO / MINHA MAIOR PAIXÃO VAMOS FLAMENGO / E ESSA TAÇA VAMOS CONQUISTAR!

(Come on Flamengo! Come on, let's be champions. Come on Flamengo – you're my biggest love. Come on Flamengo – and let's be champions!)

185

COCOCABANA

SERVES 4

Drink this and you'll be instantly transported to Copacabana beach. The combination of rum, cachaça, strawberries and coconut can't help but give you that holiday feeling, even if you're in rainy England in July.

75ml cachaça
75ml Malibu
50ml coconut cream
50ml lemon juice
50ml simple sugar syrup (page 159)
90ml pineapple juice
180ml coconut water
75ml strawberry purée (page 159)
ice cubes
1 lemon, sliced
1 orange, sliced

Pour all the ingredients except the orange and lemon slices into a large jug and stir well. Fill with ice and stir again. Top with lemon and orange slices.

INDEX

CABANA – HOW IT ALL BEGAN

★ ★

It all started with a phone call. Jamie Barber had always been captivated by *churrascarias*, or Brasilian barbecue restaurants: the ballet of waiters gliding around tables, huge skewers of freshly cooked meat, bright colours, zingy flavours and the smoke of the barbecue pit. This was always the image in his mind's eye, but when he visited them in London he found them disappointing.

He called up David Ponté, a fellow restaurateur and old friend, in February 2011 and made a simple proposition: 'What about doing Brasilian barbecue – but doing it properly?' David was born in Rio, and a childhood in the country and subsequent trips back home had always left him with a deep *saudade* – a longing and nostalgia for his memories of home. Jamie didn't have to ask him twice.

Together, they set out to create a Brasilian barbecue restaurant that would showcase the best of Brasil: the optimism, the vibrant ingredients, the spice. There would be no football, no beach bums and no girl from Ipanema. Jamie's sister Lizzy hopped aboard to whip the boys into shape, Chef Director David Rood set to work creating and testing recipes from a constant stream of ideas – and Cabana was born.